Rights, Violations, and the Contract of Free Will

Artemis Pruitt

Contents

Preface

Given the state of the modern world, it is not uncommon for many people to come to believe that the value of freedom has perhaps failed us.

But freedom has not failed us.

Instead, it is we who have failed freedom. Which is to say—we have failed to understand and appreciate the actual true logical meaning of freedom. And in turn, we have failed to realize freedom's true value and true place in society.

This matter of freedom has certainly not yet been resolved, and it remains open to be addressed.

What follows here then is a discourse—on the true nature of the meaning of freedom with respect to human existence, human rights, and being an individual in modern society...

Ownership of Rights

IN ALL MATTERS PERTAINING to the rights of man, or the rights of human beings—or, *human rights*—where governments, laws, and social contracts have long and often been said to be concerned—no concept is there more relevant and important than the concept of freedom. And yet, perhaps not so coincidentally, no concept of such esteemed social interest is there ever more commonly misrepresented and more thoroughly misconstrued.

While the *term* "freedom" has certainly suffered from no lack of popularity, its meaning proceeds to wallow in at least as much ambiguity and contradiction. What so frequently claims to epitomize the definition of the term only all too often tends to exemplify all things to the contrary—and, consequently—freedom's true place in modern society only continues to be marred by so many dubious appropriations of the term itself.

Although apprehension of only the most basic impressions of the value of freedom has, to some extent, become widely promulgated throughout some portions of the civilized nations of the world—e.g., the recognition at the very least that humanity should not tolerate the practices of slavery or genocide—*comprehension* of freedom's more

1

profound conceptual depth is still miserably lacking, if not altogether discouraged.

Rarely does there appear to be any expressed interest in further expounding upon what the word freedom actually means. The definition of freedom is rather presumed to be a matter long-since resolved, and any attempt to further pursue the subject always seems to be simply brushed off as a foregone conclusion. Thus, the progress and fruition of freedom's true value in modern society has only been hindered and impeded by complacence with the more zealous and presumptuous adaptations of the meaning of the term.

The word is habitually overburdened with negative and erroneous connotations. In many instances—acts of wild, belligerent, irresponsible, violent, oppressive, invasive, and intrusive behavior have all been consistently perceived as tantamount to exercises of "*freedom*".

Presumably, popular opinion still considers "*doing what I want*"—without any further ado—to be the premier essence of the definition of freedom. As if being collared and fettered and dragged around like some Pavlovian dog, imprisoned and enslaved by the constant and incessant commands and demands of one's physical wants, emotional urges, and mythical desires epitomized what it means to be "*free*".

As if putting forth the effort to engage any sort of logical intervention with one's physical wants, emotional urges, and mythical desires were some sort of an indictment against one's freedom, and not rather in fact the very essence of an exercise of freedom itself.

Moreover—where a particular individual might be so often occupied about the business of merely *doing what he wants*—it is not simply towards his own conscience and interventions of logic that he means contempt, but also towards the presence of other human beings and the perceived insult that *others* represent to his physical, emotional, and mythical impulses as well.

Thus, for the zealous, who become so often callous, the definition of freedom also conveniently includes the supposed "freedom" to impose their wants, whims, wishes, urges, and desires upon other people and compel others to be dragged around by the commands and demands of those very selfsame impulses as well.

And—to be sure—if you do not bow down and obey the commands and demands of the zealous and the callous, they want to accuse *you* of attacking or offending *their* supposed definition of freedom.

The meaning of freedom has always been misconstrued and misrepresented by either one (or both) of these two predominant means:

Either it is mistaken for *tyranny*—as if freedom were made to be worn like some sort of badge of supremacy, to be flashed around whenever and wherever one likes to justify imposing the perceived and supposed *supremacy* of one's physical wants, emotional urges, and mythical desires over other people.

Or else, it is confused with *truancy*—as if it were some sort of a license to exempt oneself from accountability and evade the basic responsibilities inherent to being such a rightly sovereign and independent, self-aware individual.

Of course, virtually every adult on the face of the planet would unanimously agree that they *want* freedom, or maybe even that they value freedom in the highest esteem and regard, above virtually everything else. But upon further examination, what many individuals come to prove in fact to *not want* is accountability and responsibility—the very inherent hallmarks of any true presence or presentation of freedom.

To the truant, accountability and responsibility are viewed as cumbersome chores, burdens, or *work*—veritable disruptions of the perceived unbridled freedom of their physical wants, emotional urges, and mythical desires. To such individuals, accountability and responsibility just plain reek of *effort*. And for them—effort is the *enemy* of freedom. In this sense, it becomes easier to simply lie down in the backseat and allow impulses to drive one's vehicle through life.

But it is indeed the callous tyrant, even more than the callow truant, who so comes to diminish and degrade the value of freedom the most—as tyrants are all too often found in positions of high power and authority, where they stand to do more extensive harm.

Nevertheless, both tyrant and truant alike are guilty of misusing the word to affect validation of their particular feelings of boundless entitlement. Both construe freedom as a badge of supremacy. Both *do as they want*. Both refuse accountability, and both claim exemption from any number of the responsibilities inherent to freedom—all while insisting that it is the responsibility of everyone else with whom they come into contact to cater to their every want, whim, wish, urge, or desire.

Both tyrant and truant are driven by the reckless and irresponsible belief that this is their world, and the rest of us are just expendable and subservient objects that just so happen to be living in it. Both are consumed by the wants, urges, and desires to impose supremacy and dominance over other individuals.

Both tyrant and truant expect to be served; both impose irrational demands—some more maliciously, others more passive-aggressively.

As the tyrant and the truant believe—*rights* are their wishes and your commands. Servitude and obedience to the perceived absolute and unequivocal authority of their particular impulsive demands is *your* duty and *your* obligation, and all that does not in turn comply with their demands is thus subsequently condemned and chastised for being some sort of attack or persecution against them and their supposed interpretation of the meaning of the word freedom.

What the tyrant and the truant actually come to believe is that their own "freedom" somehow includes the power to overrule, condemn, and nullify the freedom of other individuals.

One of this sort is stuck in that awkward and bizarre habit of confusing freedom with the feelings of the punitive powers of tyranny and the impunity of truancy—the very primitive and archaic inclinations that the value of freedom was indeed rightly conceptualized to overcome in the first place.

Each individual is ultimately, after all, indeed only logically *right* to come to gain freedom *from* tyranny and freedom *from* truancy. No individual is by any means ever rightly bound to serve as a prisoner or a slave to the commands and demands of another individual's wants, whims, wishes, urges, feelings, beliefs, or desires. Nor is any individual ever rightly bound to serve as a prisoner or a slave to the commands and demands of one's *own* physical, emotional, or mythical impulses.

Where any individual is simply led on the leash of impulses—whether one's own, or the impulses of others—one there literally has no logical right to stake claim to any such grasp of *freedom*.

What is further being alluded to here is our persistent failure to comprehend the real and true nature of the very meaning of the concept of freedom.

What we have repeatedly failed to understand is that freedom is in fact tantamount to *ownership*—and moreover, to the *sovereignty* of ownership.

Such that—what is truly an individual's freedom is the individual's sovereign ownership of one's very own rightly sovereign and independent being—of one's very own rightly sovereign and independent life, body, mind, conscience, ideas, identity, interests, values, tastes, tendencies, preferences, property—one's very own collective and comprehensive *rights*—those which rightly belong to one's very own sovereign and independent individual human *being*.

Where one claims ownership of freedom—one is there only really rightly claiming *ownership* of one's very own sovereign individual (human) existence. Where one claims freedom, one is there only really rightly distinguishing oneself as a sovereign representative individual claim of an ownership to freedom.

Freedom is ownership of one's own individual human existence—of one's very own rightly sovereign individual human being. Freedom is ownership of oneself. It is *not* ownership of other sovereign individuals. The definition of freedom does not mean to imply or include any such unlimited power to own, intrude, invade, or otherwise encroach upon someone else's sovereign existence and sovereign ownership of rights.

Beyond the mere ownership of any such parcel of land, the individual human being is the rightful owner of one's very own self. There is no ownership of any property of any greater value than the ownership of one's very own individual being.

Each is the only rightful owner of one's very own sovereign life, body, mind, conscience, self, identity, ideas, interests, values, property, and so forth. The individual cannot rightly claim to be free if the individual is not the rightful owner of one's very own being, life, body, mind, values, and other property. Individuals cannot rightly be said to be living in a condition of freedom where others are imposing ownership over these for them.

What then does not belong to an individual's sovereign ownership of rights cannot rightly be said to belong to the individual's freedom. Thus, the individual cannot rightly claim to be *free* to own, invade, or otherwise encroach upon someone else's life, body, mind, values, interests, property, etc. The very essence of the value of an individual's freedom is one's very own sovereign and independent ownership of rights.

Furthermore, each individual is a sovereign and independent *experience* of (human) *being*. Each individual's experience of existence is an independent experience. No individual can ever actually truly experience another individual's experience of existence. And no individual can thus ever rightly claim to *own* the experience of another individual's existence.

This is not to suggest in any way that we are all such lone and disconnected islands of existence, incapable of sharing information about our experiences in order to gain mutual understanding and encourage the growth and development of comprehensive knowledge. But is that not the very fundamental purpose of ation anyway, after all?

But it is simply not enough and not even accurate to say that each individual is just a separate physical body sharing in one and the same absolute experience of existence. Rather—more than a mere objective piece of meat—each individual human being is here only rightly representative of a certain individual experience of a certain sovereign existence, life, body, mind, conscience, identity, behaviors, ideas, interests, values, and property of one's very own.

And as such, each is the only rightful sole, sovereign, and accountable *owner* of the rights belonging to one's very own being—those of one's very own sovereign and independent life, body, mind, conscience, behaviors, ideas, interests, values, property, and so forth.

Each individual thus only has right to lay claim to freedom about that which only rightly belongs to one's very own sovereign ownership of rights. Therefore, one individual's *freedom* (or, sovereign *ownership of rights*) cannot then rightly be said to own, contain, or otherwise invade, intrude, or encroach upon another individual's freedom (another individual's sovereign ownership of rights).

Thus, one individual cannot rightly claim to own any such "freedom" over that which is not rightly his or her's to own—namely here, the sovereignty of another individual.

Each individual is also further right to recognize oneself as being representative of a sole, sovereign, and independent individual *constitution* of (human) being—as *one* distinct and distinguished constitution of human being—as one "configuration" of human—as one individual constitution of human being in societal communication with other individual constitutions of human being.

Here then, as being representative of just such a rightly sovereign and independent constitution of being, each individual is thus indeed right to come to know oneself and represent oneself in human society as a *free will*—i.e., a sole, sovereign, and independent *individual (human) will*—in contractual society with other sole, sovereign, and independent individual human wills.

Freedom is thus essentially our first right—our quintessential right. We are here indeed rightly responsible for coming to realize and recognize our rightful sovereignty and independence as human individuals.

Each is here right indeed to be accountable for oneself as a sovereign and independent individual human being, and to fulfill the necessary and inherent responsibilities conducive to maintaining one's very own sovereign and independent ownership of being.

Each is here further right to engage the logical efforts necessary to come to gain the wits of self-awareness and self-governance. Each is here further right to mature and evolve and develop a conscience and consensus of logic in which, with which, and through which to come to further gain and improve upon comprehensive knowledge—to ascertain truths, facts, and rights about this individual experience of human being. Each is right to hold court over so many physical sensations, emotional feelings, and mythical beliefs. Each is right to come to know oneself as a sovereign and independent ownership of rights, and to further represent oneself as a sovereign and independent constitution of being—as a *free will*—in society with other individuals.

As such, there can hardly be any right more unanimous and universal than the right of freedom.

Anywhere an individual would otherwise mean to deny accountability and responsibility for oneself, either explicitly or implicitly, to deny the very value of being such a rightly responsible and accountable, sovereign and independent ownership of an individual human existence, we should there immediately recognize such an individual to be in contempt and denial of the very intrinsic and imperative value of freedom itself.

We can there only be left to inquire as to whom or what is then rightly accountable and responsible for such an individual?

Many such denials and deferrals of accountability and responsibility go to even further extremes and are not only condoned by many in society, but rather even come to be celebrated as acts of "freedom" themselves.

In other words—individuals who refuse the efforts of accountability and responsibility are actually awarded the label of freedom for so doing. Such individuals are there, in effect, being awarded a claim to a freedom to act *in contempt* of freedom—or to act in denial of freedom.

But how can acts of *anti-freedom* possibly be celebrated as exemplary of freedom itself? Is someone also considered "smart" who acts in contempt of intelligence?

Consider the weight of that.

But indeed—as far as sane, viable, individual human beings go—freedom is a responsibility. It is the quintessence of responsibilities. Freedom is responsibility of ownership, and freedom is ownership of responsibility—for oneself, for one's own being, and for one's own sovereign and independent ownership of rights.

It is only then rightly and logically incumbent upon each individual to come to know one's very own rightly sovereign and independent constitution of human being as a free will—and to come forth and stand as the only logical and rightful sole, sovereign, and independent owner, executor, and representative of one's very own free will.

Of a certain sovereign mind, conscience, sense, faculties, and consensus of logic, each sane, viable individual human being is here indeed only rightly responsible for coming to know, comprehend, realize, respect, and appreciate the true meaning of one's very own rightly sovereign and independent ownership of rights as the rightful expression of one's very own freedom.

Furthermore, to come to know any rights at all, an individual must be of such a sovereign knowing mind, conscience, sense, faculties, and consensus of logic in order to logically and rightly evaluate and determine any such rights whatsoever. Otherwise, lacking such a sovereign conscience and the necessary faculties of logic through which to appeal in order to determine rights, one cannot rightly be said to be sufficiently equipped to ascertain what is even right at all. One would here only be acting in constant contempt of logic and freedom.

Short of logic, one is always, in the end, only inevitably controlled by some form of tyranny or another.

Freedom and right are ultimately very much in fact logical intellectual concepts—and as such, we are only severely lost and deluded if we live under the presumption that any-one's wants, whims, wishes, urges, feelings, beliefs, or desires ever rightly decides, determines, justifies, or adjudicates any real and true knowledge of any some such *right* or *freedom* at all, in sheer spite and contempt of logic.

Only rather by sovereign and conscious interventions of logic do concepts such as freedom and right then ever become truly ascertained, rightly adjudicated, or further *known*.

Of course, each individual does indeed have limita-tions—but only rightly his or her very own sovereign limita-tions—of his or her very own sovereign body, mind, knowl-edge, talents, abilities, etc. No individual here ever rightly imposes the limitations of these over another. The limita-tions of one individual's will are not for another individual to decide. Thus, it is imperative that each individual come to know each's very own sovereign limitations and know them well.

It has only ever been an egregious error to construe free will as if it would mean to imply a will *"without limitations"*, or a will of *endless power*.

But if each individual is truly free, each is here only rightly accounting for oneself as representative of a sole, sovereign individual ownership of rights—of a certain sole, sovereign *individual* experience of human being.

The individual does not here then rightly construe free-dom as if to count oneself as *limitless*. One here instead rightly counts oneself as *one*—as one sovereign and inde-pendent individual experience of human being—as one sov-ereign and independent individual *owner*ship of rights—as one sovereign and independent representative individual constitution of being, distinct and distinguished from any and all other individuals with which one is here involved in contractual society.

An individual human being does indeed have every logical right to come to know oneself as a sovereign and independent individual human being—apt and fit to represent oneself in human society as a sovereign and independent individual human *will* of one's own—free and independent of any and all other human wills with which one is here involved in societal communication.

Indeed, we are many different and distinct individual human beings, and where the interests and behaviors of human beings are concerned, there is certainly not but one single absolute right way to live. Human beings are a plural, diverse, kinetic, and complex species—availed to many different, diverse, kinetic, and complex experiences. Thus, we are constituted of many different, diverse, kinetic, and complex ideas, interests, values, behaviors, traits, characteristics, and so forth.

What rights each individual will come to know will only rightly come to occur to one's very own sovereign and independent conscience and logical account, out of one's very own sovereign and independent individual experience of human being, as one's very own sovereign and independent rights. One could not otherwise rightly claim to know much by simply deferring one's will and one's freedom to the prejudices and presumptions of some form of tyranny thrown upon us by others.

One cannot rightly expect to gain anything genuine at all in spite of one's very own sovereign and independent individual efforts.

Surely then, the concept of freedom, the very profound meaning of freedom, and the very real and true value of freedom are at least worthy of some investigation, if not perhaps a little redress from time to time.

We should think these matters are far from deserving of simply being written off as foregone conclusions, and we should think the many prejudices and presumptions and misconceptions and misconstructions laid upon the lap of freedom are at least due for a little dusting off every once in awhile.

Thus here, the meaning of freedom—now as always—begs our further inquiries...

Wild vs. Free

WE HAVE LONG BEEN stuck in the habit of presuming that freedom is the condition of nature into which humans and all other animals were supposedly born. This essentially amounts to mean that we presume "wild" and "free" are synonymous terms. But as such, our presumptions are wildly incorrect. *Wild* and *Free* are rather in fact two very different and distinct concepts, which do not necessarily, nor necessarily often, coincide.

A little wild bird or a little wild rodent, forced to live enslaved by constant fear, panic, and anxiety—always skittish and quivering and jerking about—constantly having to look over its shoulder before taking each nibble of even the tiniest morsel of food, perpetually fettered with the terror that each nibble it attempts might very well be its last, if such an opportunistic predator happens along at just the right moment to seize upon the advantage of even the slightest lapse of alertness—can hardly be justified in laying such a pitiful little definition upon the heavy shoulders of a term as that such as the likes of *freedom*.

Any bird or rodent or any other animal, including a human, who might live in such "natural" conditions as those of the wild must there only be living in a type of condition

15

as to be constantly constrained and imprisoned by the many impending, intrusive, and invasive circumstances that just such a wild and natural environment brings to offer. And indeed, as we have previously alluded, such a wild animal is there also living imprisoned and enslaved by the incessant commands and demands of its very own physical, emotional, and mythical impulses.

Hence, the wild is a place where any individual of any particular species is not only constrained by the impotence and insecurities of its own physical, emotional, and mythical impulses, but also by the wild and not-so-interested-in-freedom circumstances imminent about just such a wild and natural environment—lethal predators, voracious scavengers, pesky rodents, pernicious pests, and an endless cast of various other strange and peculiar animals and all the imposing and irrational physical, emotional, and mythical baggage they bring to paradise—in addition to the countless numbers of microbes, pathogens, parasites, viruses, bacteria, deadly diseases, venomous species, and poisonous substances—as well as the severe and ever-erratic weather conditions, extreme temperature changes, climate fluctuations, atmospheric threats and geological events, topographical impasses, toxified bodies of water, intermittent deficiencies and excesses of water, stinginess and scarcity of plant resources...

Nope—the wild is certainly no place of business conducive to the interests of freedom.

Freedom, as we should well know by now, is a very profound and highly sophisticated concept—requisite of efforts, faculties, and processes of only the most astute logical order. Hence, matters of freedom are certainly no place of business for wild animals—nor, for that matter, any domesticated animals—dogs and cats, for example.

To that end—lions and tigers and bears, moose and mice and geese, hyenas and javelinas and amoebas, all appear to have no immediate or discernable interest in any of our logical discussions about freedom, rights, ownership, laws, or the sovereignty of individuals. Our interpretations of these wild critters and their inner-workings notwithstanding, we have as yet to make any headway in terms of impressing any notion about the value of freedom upon them.

Perhaps the zealot—one amongst those who so casually insists to imply that *wild* and *free* are synonymous terms—would be interested in serving as liaison between us and the lions to see where we might stand upon any sort of mutual agreement as to the value of freedom and the sovereignty of individuals?

Although, the zealot will of course want to be swift and efficient about getting our point across, since—as we have come to be informed—lions are known to sleep in excess of 20 hours a day. So in the short window that is the remaining 4 hours—if the lions are not busy hunting, killing, eating, drinking, shitting, pissing, or procreating—they very likely will not have much time left over in their busy schedules to concern themselves with any such matters of "freedom".

But the zealot should not be deterred.

We will remind him before his meeting that lions are not only extremely lazy, but also quite cowardly—so he should be fine.

In the interim, the zealot will likely continue to insist that we should come to look upon such wild animals and admire how they are so "*free*"—how they are so "unbridled" and "unrestrained" and "unrestricted"—and how they have "no limitations"—

Wait—what? *No limitations?*

Wild animals have plenty of limitations!

For one—most of them appear to have absolutely no sense of humor whatsoever. So right out of the gate, I'd say that's a pretty severe limitation already.

Strike one.

Also, their ability to *create*—the very fundamental and essential premise and purpose of freedom at all—is, at best—extremely limited, if not completely non-existent.

Strike two.

And, their particular senses of logic are so obviously deficient as to be rendered woefully askew—or else they are entirely absent altogether.

Strike three!

Most wild animals instead appear to have no care or concern at all for the efforts necessary to emancipate themselves from the enslavement to their physical wants, emotional urges, and mythical desires—enough to come to see these for the severe constraints and limitations that they truly are. Many also do not appear to be inclined enough to develop a conscience and consensus of logic—enough to overcome the brutal, barbaric, and irrational ways of the wild—enough to conduct such a logical court of appeal in which to oversee the many wild and irrational physical, emotional, and mythical impulses—enough to exhibit sovereignty and independence and to be accountable and responsible for their own physical, emotional, and mythical impulses—enough to conduct themselves as such rightly sovereign and independent individuals, fit and able to participate in such necessarily logical contractual social agreements, as we humans are so fit and able to do.

So we see, in fact, in so many ways, the natural ways of the wild and the ways of wild animals are actually very much indeed wrought with constraints and restrictions. Very much in contempt of freedom. Very much askew of logic. Very little ado about creating. Very much ado about destruction.

For any animal, wild or domesticated—human or otherwise—to simply act and react about the Pavlovian confines of merely doing what one's physical wants, emotional urges, and mythical desires compel—or to merely act and react within the confines of what the physical, emotional, and mythical impulses of other individuals dictate—is not in any way worthy or deserving of being considered "*free*".

The notion that any man or any other animal of nature was ever born into a condition of freedom is fallacious indeed, but so too, however, we modern humans continue to prove that we have no right to claim that we have satisfied the meaning of the term either. We most certainly have *not* succeeded hitherto with respect to fulfilling the promise of freedom.

In fact, more often than we may want to care to admit, many humans have been continuing to show signs of regression.

Consider for a moment—what could possibly be the intent of those who seriously put forth the proposition, whether explicitly or implicitly, that people need *less* freedom?

As if what people really need is *less* independence? As if what people really need is *less* responsibility? *Less* accountability? *Less* maturity? Less development of logic and intellect and *more* of the same old primitive and archaic physical, emotional, and mythical impulses?

Is this merely strange—or is there something far more deranged going on here?

Human beings are most assuredly not born into a condition of freedom, but every human being is in fact born with a brain and a certain degree of potential—and for that—all that most human beings really lack is effort. And more specifically—conscious efforts of logic.

We are all adults here, one would presume, and suffice it to say—we should owe no apologies for that.

Most among the wild animals, though, obviously have very little to no respect at all for accountability, personal responsibility, logical maturity, and the value of individual sovereignty. Wild animals have not engaged the efforts necessary to evolve a sufficient enough, nor even remarkably similar enough sense of logic, as humans have, through which to comprehend, appreciate, and improve upon the value of freedom. They tend to rather express very little interest in logic at all—let alone express any extended interest in further comprehending the very profound logical meaning of freedom.

Those of the wild are instead captivated and held hostage—imprisoned in that dangerous subconscious playground, where physical wants and emotional urges become personified, and so often deified, as the archetypical roles of predators and prey, masters and slaves, lords and servants are portrayed and enacted and run amuck in a cacophony of—*do what I want!, do as I say!, serve me!, obey me!, I'm up-you're down!, kill or be killed!, fight or flight!*—manifestations of fear, panic, terror, guilt, anxiety, and insecurity—in utter contempt of logic and coherence, contempt of accountability and responsibility, and contempt of freedom, independence, and the sovereignty of individuals and their rightfully sovereign and independent ownerships of rights.

In the wild though, everything tends to be a provocation for violence.

Plenty of wild animals are indulged with an overabundance of power and are yet devoid of any appreciable interest in freedom. We have indeed seen far too many examples of this throughout our own human history—up to and including those that continue to persist throughout the world today—in addition to those which have presented themselves to us through our observations of so many wild and domesticated animals.

These should present more than sufficient evidence of the fact that freedom and power also do *not* mean the same.

Wild animals do not fight for freedom. Wild animals instead fight for supremacy and survival. On face value, these may seem like natural and innocuous enough instincts—but where any particular rogue and insecure animal has come to find itself indulged with a certain degree of power, the physical want, emotional urge, and mythical desire for supremacy only far too easily and often comes to manifest itself in the form of a dangerous tyrant, along with all the horrific consequences that such a tyrant's impulses bring others to bear.

Indeed, we have seen far too much ado about tyranny and truancy and far too little ado about sovereignty and independence among individuals of any particular species of animal. But we should only therefore be reminded of the perpetual proof that tyranny and truancy are very much in fact two sides of the very same coin. Both exist very much symbiotically—in sheer spite, contempt, and consternation of freedom and the responsibilities thereof. Also very much in sheer spite, contempt, and consternation of accountability, logic, and the development of the intellect. Also very much in contempt and consternation of the profound responsibilities of logic to hold court and keep so many irrational wants, whims, wishes, urges, feelings, beliefs, and desires at bay.

We know these patterns of behavior all too well by now. We have seen them over and over and over again, throughout the entire course of human history. We have seen and heard the repeated insistence over and over again that what people really need to do is continuously turn the clocks backward and spit in the face of logic over and over again—and constantly revert back to the impulses of the wild—and repeat the same mistakes of history over and over again, in spite of our profound logical advancements to know better. As if human knowledge has not already improved, matured, and evolved, through so many efforts and exercises of logic, far beyond what any of these could have ever presumed to know.

We should not have to play coy about this. We should know very well by now that we are logically fit and able to better ourselves and learn from the mistakes of human history. And we have learned quite enough from the vile and atrocious mistakes laid bare in those bloody tracks already. We know that it is indeed our very inherent responsibility to, in fact—*know better*. We know that it is our very inherent responsibility to exercise our logic and improve upon knowledge—to evolve and *do better* than what our physically

22

violent, emotionally-charged, myth-fueled human predecessors had done.

Again, we know these patterns. They are all too familiar to us by now. But those do indeed harken back to the ways of the wild. The wild *is* a place of war—of constant battles for supremacy and survival, fueled by such physical wants, emotional urges, and mythical desires. Much to the detriment and degradation of logic—much to the detriment and degradation of any remarkable interest in freedom.

It is rather in fact through efforts, exercises, and the ongoing development of our very own conscience and consensus of logic that we so come to improve and evolve—and, in conjunction with our opposable thumbs—that we so come to create the artifacts pertinent to furthering our abilities through which to continue to improve and evolve.

Our logic is thus in fact the key which opens the door to our freedom, through which we are able to become such self-aware individuals, and to further create and improve and mature and evolve.

Our logic is thus also what truly sets us apart from the other animals.

Be assured though—other animals do indeed have eyes and nervous systems and brains, or some comparable masses thereof—so, yes indeed—they most certainly do experience physical sensations, emotional feelings, and to be sure—mythical *beliefs*. Emotionally-charged, visually apparitional mythical scenarios do so indeed run through the minds of other animals, to varying degrees of occupation.

Observe the behavior of the sleeping dog caught up in a bit of a lucid dream for a glimpse into the mythos of other animals.

Perhaps this might also lend some explanation as to why lions spend so much time sleeping—maybe their subconscious is busy entertaining themselves with certain scenarios of such delusional grandeur.

What wild animals instead *lack* is an appreciable court and consensus of logic—in which and through which to ascertain knowledge and adjudicate rights. They lack a higher court of appeal—a court of *logic*—in which to bring physical sensations, emotional feelings, and mythical beliefs to be examined and evaluated for truth, knowledge, and further *rightness*.

But, to be sure—while many species of wild animals are obviously askew of logic, and what many species of wild animals lack with respect to the interests of freedom—they do indeed make up for in the interests of tenacity and survival. Some do tend to be so extremely tenacious, resilient, and cunning in ways—far beyond our means—that can easily bring a lump to a grown man's throat.

But let us just quickly clarify what is meant here—

Homo sapiens sapiens is not a subspecies cut out for long-tenured endurance. We are not sharks, cockroaches, or tardigrades. As far as species go, we are not so invincible. In fact, if truth be told—in terms of raw physical and emotional fortitude—pound for pound—we are among the more frail, fragile, and wimpier of earth's species, in spite of our esteemed position in the food chain.

But this is by no means in any way meant to be a statement of a whimper. No intent is made here to glorify any species—let alone some nasty cockroach. This is simply meant to state that there are those other species of animals, who for instance—when they lose a limb, just grow a new one back in its place. Or others—when the particular need arises, simply signal their entire bodies to blend in and camouflage themselves into the scape of their surroundings. Some walk through a forest engulfed in flames and come out the other side without seeming to have even noticed the smoke. Some, when they are "done" with their old outer membranes, just grow new ones back in their places and let the old ones lay on the ground, like so many used sweaters.

By contrast—our veneers, prosthetics, and ghillie suits are not so impressive.

We humans tend too easily to overlook the specific animal efforts involved in such talents of the wild—especially about those who have really honed and sharpened their skills. Out of arrogance, humans like to disregard the talents of other species and brush them off as mere *accidents* of nature—or worse, relegate other animals to the position of mindless puppets and pretend that their actions are simply being controlled by some version of a grand anthropomorphic puppet master.

So to simply discount these strangely sophisticated talents of so many wild animals as mere dumb accidents or as the makings of some anthropomorphic deity is indeed far too zealous and shortsighted. But these talents of other species should not be presumed to occur as acts of their own *immediate* "conscious" design, either. A wild animal certainly does not just wake up one morning and decide to spontaneously sprout wings and fly any more than does a human. The efforts and processes and amount of time required to produce even the slightest of evolutionary changes is far beyond the capacity, ability, or duration of any one single individual's lifetime, of this species or any other.

We humans though, *are* indeed conscious animals after all, and even if we cannot literally and spontaneously spring our bodies into flight, we are at least consciously aware of the concepts of freedom and evolution and the ability of a species to effect improvements and evolve—even if many of us are not willing to exert the logical efforts necessary to achieve a sufficient grasp of the real and true implications of human evolution.

But as to what extent we can say that other animals, especially wild animals, apprehend any inkling of a concept such as freedom—or, furthermore "consciously" apprehend *any* concept at all—is not in our wildest dreams even remotely available to us at the present time.

Whatever senses these animals have, even those we would like to correlate with our sense of logic, these are evidently not committed to any interest in freedom—at least not in any paramount or well-developed capacity anyway. Freedom, in the wild, is not so remarkable a priority. Freedom is a value rather more of interest to a species of individuals inclined towards creative purposes—and not so much to those species predominantly only interested in supremacy and survival.

If other species of animals even remotely entertain any sense akin to logic whatsoever, it certainly does not exist in any paramount position—where it rightfully belongs in rational beings, such as humans, to rightfully appeal to for truth and hold court over the other unqualified senses.

For those other animal species of the wild—physical sensations, emotional urges, and mythical desires clearly overrule any semblance of any sort of logic or rationality, or any further interest in the value of freedom whatsoever.

But whether Pavlov's dogs or Schrödinger's cats, none of us can deny that we do in fact absorb sensory information. And indeed, we all do transmit and communicate the effects of processing so many waves of information right back out through our bodies for others to receive. We can and should infer *some* similarities, so as to promote further understanding, so that comprehensive knowledge may indeed continue to prosper, develop, improve, mature, and evolve.

We can and should also appreciate the vast complexity of our differences. No two species are the same, and no two individuals within any given species are the same—especially within a species as complex, diverse, and creative as our own. Our complex, diverse, and creative differences, in fact, only serve to provide valuable insight and further improve upon our comprehensive knowledge of all that we are able to experience throughout the profound pluralistic nature of this existence. To otherwise pretend life to be so simple, uniform, and predetermined is indeed a naive and grievous error—and one well beyond its expiration date.

As for the tenacious, the resilient, and the strangely-sophisticated—those at least shed some light on the great and exotic potential of what a species can and may become fit enough to endure. What peculiar and intriguing talents these wild animals exhibit and exude is almost always captivating and impressive enough to generate at least a certain degree of humility.

But we too have our dignity. We humans have our own talents to tend to. We have our own creative senses of logic and our own opposable thumbs.

The sharks, cockroaches, and tardigrades—those among the most enduring of the wild—do indeed have their own talents, and their own senses, and their own interests, and their own needs, and their own ways—some we may find awe-inspiring, and some we may find just downright awful. For our own present purposes and future causes, we can at least observe, interpret, and infer what these wild and phenomenal talents have been so developed to accomplish.

What evolutionary changes a species can and may provoke certainly relates much to their particular circumstances and priorities, but the fact that a species can and may indeed provoke certain courses of change within itself and its kind has become quite evident and clear to us by now. Some species will provoke changes of a more sudden and immediate order, while others may only provoke changes of a more gradual and subtle variety, if even any remarkable changes at all. Humans always seem to want to agitate towards urgency. But such is the trade-off for a supposedly awesome brain—more frail physicality, more fragile emotionality, and more docile mythicality. Thus, we *require* more intellectual effort.

We are not cockroaches. Ours is not the course of steadfast, long-tenured, hard-armored endurance. Humans are not fit and equipped for hundreds of millions of years of tenacity. We *have to* evolve. Change, adapt, modify, improve, evolve; change, adapt, modify, improve, evolve—this is our course. We cycle through changes to effect improvements.

We certainly do not look much like our past or future selves. But at least we are aware of this—or, at least, we *should* be aware of this by now. We have been becoming more aware of this, through so many contributive efforts of logic—aware of our evolution, aware of our past, present, and further potential to continue to change, adapt, modify, improve, and evolve. And we have indeed evolved and developed our specifically human intellect, conscience, and consensus of logic in order to gain the creative independence through which to cause so many circumstances here to improve.

Again—we are not lions or tigers or bears. We do not in any right frame of mind make decisions and resolve our conflicts by battling to see whose teeth and claws and muscle power will reign supreme and thus become anointed as the chosen ones to inseminate the females. But in the wild, conflicts are indeed persistently resolved by just such brute displays of power. But if a human can develop a mind to become aware of such behaviors, then one can certainly develop a mind through which to emancipate oneself from just such animalistic impulses and inclinations and continue to further improve and evolve.

Without logic and opposable thumbs, even the strongest of men among us would be no match for even the weakest of lions or tigers or bears. But that need not be of any consequence to us. We are rational beings who have indeed evolved the conscience, consensus of logic, and opposable thumbs conducive to the interests of freedom. We certainly do not rightly adjudicate truth, rights, and laws out of animalistic impulses—of any physical, emotional, or mythical kind. We only rightly ascertain and adjudicate truth, rights, and laws *with logic*, in the interests of freedom.

Homo sapiens sapiens is a subspecies fit enough to exert the logical efforts necessary to mature and evolve beyond the many imposing and intrusive, self-destructive ways of the wild. We are fit enough to emancipate ourselves from being overruled by such primitive and archaic animalistic wants, urges, and desires. We are fit enough to intervene and hold court with a consensus of logic. We are fit enough to further realize the greater value of such a logical, accountable, responsible, creative, and genuine life of independence, in which to further overcome the unjust tyrannies as those of the wild.

So says the sane, viable, logical human to the wild:

"This is unacceptable! I don't have to live like this! I have a sovereign mind to improve my circumstances and create my own improvements..."

Much like a spider, a human being is indeed capable of shedding that cumbersome old barbaric nonsense of the wild and leaving it to lie like so much of a used sweater.

But such realizations will have to be achieved on sovereign and independent individual courses of maturity, on a broader course of further evolution of the human species, on a course of realizing the errors of so many primitive and archaic prejudices and presumptions and molting them for new and improved, more honest skins—each to one's own talents and limitations, each to one's own species, each to one's own individual self.

Let the sharks and cockroaches and tardigrades go on with their own talents and their own fittings and their own ways.

We humans will move on now and take a look at an example of one of our little mirrors...

Birth of the Individual

THAT TO WHICH, FOR which, and about which the value of freedom necessarily pertains—or indeed, must have ever been conceived to have any meaning whatsoever—is in fact, the individual human being itself. But the naive suggestion that a human being is in any way ever "born free" is not only profoundly misleading, it is just downright false.

Far too much is there left to be implied that freedom is such an absolute and innate condition which an individual has already satisfied before birth. But the condition of a human being at birth is nothing that it will be bound to remain.

Upon birth, a human is already here imprisoned by the severe limitations of his own physical body, held at the mercy of so many spontaneous and extreme emotional fluctuations, and about to become captivated and taken hostage by those burgeoning mythical scenarios that even many adults will never come to terms with. It is all an infant can do but to cry and wail for *want* of freedom.

Anywhere it has ever been suggested that a human being is *born free*, this must only presumably be referring to the visually obvious physical body which gets passed around the hospital delivery room like so much of a hot potato. But surely adults of even the slightest notion could not possibly expect this helpless little spud to be considered a conclusive or even remotely respectable representation of the definition of *freedom*, could they?

Let us assume not.

To say that a human being is born free is really no different than suggesting that a human being is born mature. Such a proposition has always been far too zealous and presumptuous, and really, in fact—quite ridiculous. An individual has to become responsible, become independent, become a sovereign ownership of rights—he most certainly is not born that way.

At birth, this little potato still has a long way to cook before it is ready to sit at the table of society.

At birth, the individual still has much yet left ahead of him to improve upon and through which to come to better himself, and to further come to mature and evolve. Such processes will require a tremendous amount of effort on his part—as well as a great deal of time and patience.

More precise then would it be to say that an individual is born *for* freedom—to *become* free—to exert the necessary individual efforts through which to emancipate himself from the impulsive confines of his own physical wants, emotional urges, and mythical desires—to exert the necessary efforts through which to come to develop his very own conscience and consensus of logic—and to thereby come to cause and create and fulfill his very own sovereign and independent interests, intentions, causes, purposes—and further, *rights*.

An individual otherwise only does so much more of a tragic disservice to himself to simply consign himself and his great potential for freedom into the waiting hands of some tyrant who is far more interested in supremacy and dominance than in sovereignty and independence.

Independence is precisely what the child lacks, and thus precisely what any logically-minded parent should therefore only necessarily be so qualified and equipped to foster and encourage.

Independence is really what distinguishes maturity from immaturity. To mature is to become independent. And to become independent is the very essence of realizing the true nature of freedom.

All that discounts and diminishes the value of this very simple fact is the lack of appreciation of the true meaning of freedom and independence.

Here again, complacence with so many negative and erroneous connotations attached to these terms has only served to impede any further comprehension of their more profound meaning.

Far too many adults have instead adopted an entirely up-side-down, backwards, or inside-out understanding of the meaning of freedom and independence. Many adults carry such a naive impression about these terms as to look upon young children running wild and screaming at the play-ground as examples of freedom and independence at play. Examples, which in reality, befit terms precisely the *opposite* of freedom and independence.

Young children are just simply *not* independent. Young children are far too immature to be accountable for them-selves and the responsibilities conducive to being indepen-dent individuals. For where a child lacks maturity, lacks re-sponsibility, lacks accountability, lacks respect for his own sovereignty, or lacks respect for the sovereignty of others—he does indeed lack independence—and he does indeed therefore lack freedom.

And, to be sure—where any *adult* lacks maturity, responsibility, accountability, and respect for the sovereignty of oneself, as well as the sovereignty of others—he or she likewise lacks the right to claim to be acting in the interests of freedom.

It has only all too often tended to occur that an individual will simply affix the label "free" to himself, only to—in the very next move—simply throw responsibility and accountability right out the window—thus demonstrating that he believes he has declared a freedom *from* responsibility and accountability—where he has only really there, even if only unwittingly, *negated* any logical semblance of freedom altogether.

But we know all about the zealous and the presumptuous already. We know all about the callous and the callow. And we know all about the ways of tyranny and truancy.

We are by now all too familiar with such types and their denials of accountability and responsibility. They are presumably only alluding to what it was perhaps like for them when they were children—when for instance, if they were hungry—they could just pound their fists on the table, and an adult would bring them food. And if they didn't like their vegetables, they could just throw their plates on the floor, and some adult could just go ahead and clean up that mess.

When emotions and beliefs well-up and make irrational demands and dictate an individual's behavior—and then in turn—one simply transfers and imposes these burdens upon others—thus serving to only so thoroughly *depend* upon others and their efforts—in sheer spite and contempt of accountability and responsibility for one's own behavior—that's what the tyrant and the truant would really want us to believe the definition of freedom to be?

Worse yet—there appears to be very little interest, if any, in correcting these egregious misrepresentations of freedom. It would seem as though most people are perfectly okay with accepting such behaviors as valid expressions of the meaning of freedom. Even many involved in the intellectual community and persons in leadership roles seem quite content to go along with this notion that freedom simply means *doing what I want*, without any further ado.

But again—we are all adults here, presumably. We should know very well by now that a supposed "freedom" from responsibility is really no such freedom at all. We should know very well that declaring a freedom *from* responsibility really only amounts to a declaration of a supposed "freedom" to be *absolved of* freedom.

Such is obviously only a ridiculous contradiction of logic—a nullification—a *negation* of freedom. We adults should indeed expect other adults to know better.

At birth though, for his part, the infant human has not yet matured enough to know better. So he has a valid excuse. He has not yet begun to develop the wits enough to comprehend the logic of sovereignty and independence. Freedom has not yet entered his vocabulary. It will not be long, however, before our inferential minds will become aware of his initial apprehensions and inclinations *toward* freedom. Soon he will be a toddler, and he will lash out in three-alarm fits and tantrums, in sheer and apparent contempt of his *lack* of independence and lack of fitness for freedom.

But here—this should not be construed to imply that the newborn child in any way apprehends any sort of *thing* called "freedom". Nor should this be construed to suggest in any way that freedom is any sort of object, just waiting out there for him to discover it. The child is thoroughly unaware of what provokes him, and thus subsequently, of how to contend with his provocations.

His is a burgeoning dilemma, though. He will have much time left yet to develop awareness, to mature, and to further comprehend the many apprehensive physical sensations, emotional feelings, and mythical beliefs that will happen to occur throughout his experience of existence. He will have much time left yet to develop the faculties of logic through which to come to gain the wits of independence—and to further comprehend such an important concept as that of *freedom*.

Perhaps by this account, the newborn child's conundrum is only slightly more difficult than our own. We cannot rightly convey the complexity and importance of the value of freedom all at once—nor even in any especially elementary manner. So for that, many individuals simply refuse to engage and commit the efforts necessary to endeavor such a course of comprehension and further maturation. But while it may be easier to live by the impulses of wants, whims, wishes, and desires, the results are not so easy on the palate of humanity.

But freedom requires effort.

Logical comprehension of such profound concepts as freedom and independence are indeed requisite of intensive and persistent logical efforts—and we already know how truancy and tyranny feel about effort. The same as they feel about true freedom. Tyranny wants to destroy it, and truancy wants no part of it.

Concepts such as freedom also do not cater so much to the cushy comforts of basic sensory apprehension. Freedom is not among the variety of things that sit still long enough for us to at least take a picture or measure. But aren't we all most certainly apprehensive when faced with the prospect of constraints and restrictions! Enough to at least provoke a sense of aspiration *towards* the notion of freedom.

So, for us—indeed, as much as for the child—freedom is thus also most assuredly a *spirit*.

However, one would be in error here to infer any suggestion of some sort of ghost, or even a simple feeling, or any other some such thing.

Spirit is more of an expression of becoming—the burgeoning phases and phenomena of the experience of existence, of which we are so apt and willing to produce.

To be sure—*spirit* is an expression of *potential*, and—from the very literal and symbolic moment when the cord is cut—the newborn child, more than just a metaphorical potato or a simple fleshy animal, more than a mere superficial body, but not yet apt enough to call his own—becomes now an *individual* among us—and the spirit of freedom is at least as available to him as we have made any some such freedom available to ourselves.

The newborn child indeed at least now becomes representative of an individual human being, but his being is here—at present—most assuredly anything *but* free. The inevitable burdens that other humans will eventually bring to his doorstep notwithstanding, he has his own immediate and personal shortcomings here to contend with and surmount.

Here imprisoned at the mercy of his physical, emotional, mythical, and various other sensical deficiencies, disturbances, and distractions—he has neither developed a discernible conscience nor the adept discretionary faculties of logic necessary to offer any kind of doubt and contest, to inquire and investigate, to distinguish and discern much of anything about this current barrage of incoming information he is now faced with.

He is but a becoming—a burgeoning development of a complex of complex senses—"he" is caught up in the wash. *He* is relatively helpless and powerless. He can do little more than be bombarded, flooded, irked, provoked, and overwhelmed—up from the depths within—in from many there-withouts—as well as at the stint of some dubious and kinetic nowandabout—unable to "make sense" of it all.

The child can do little more than serve time as a prisoner and a slave to no real particular captor and master but to his own immediate presence and his own present deficiencies. He has not yet developed the abilities through which to come to intervene and assert himself.

While at once being piqued and pleased and uneased by streams and waves of so many strange and unfamiliar sights, sounds, tastes, touches, and smells—pushed and pulled by these and those restless and erratic emotional fluctuations—captivated and mesmerized by vague and apparent apparitions engaged in dubious theatrics, and shamed as yet by so many involuntary and uncontrollable shittings and pissings—he cannot "come to his senses" enough to emancipate himself from all of this.

His station unto himself is here inundated with conflict. His is but a veritable warzone of tugs and pushes and pulls. And he is not just some passive observer stuck in the middle, simply watching it all happen. He is a tug—and then a push—and then a pull. He is a kinetic locale of conflict and becoming. He is an unwitting host for photon parades, hormone parties, bacteria colonies, synaptic fireworks, emotional outbursts and mood swings, soothing and piercing audible waves, carnivals of flavors, tangible stings, pangs, prongs, cradles, scaldings and coolings, olfactory intakes and emissions...

Arms flailing, legs kicking, eyes blinking, mouth drooling, slobbering, teetering and tottering, weebling and wobbling, crying, sobbing, wailing, fits of giggling—he cannot stand, let alone walk—he cannot hold a spoon, let alone feed himself—he can barely chew on a crayon, let alone draw with one—he cannot speak—he cannot wash himself—he cannot protect himself—he is fragile—he is thoroughly dependent...

Nope—there's no sign of freedom here! This kid is a mess!

His self is as much a plurality as his moods and outbursts and daydreams. But having not yet developed any such remarkable sense of self-awareness, he is not really so much of a self yet at all, but indeed only so much more of a burgeoning and a becoming—a *spirit*—a spirited expression of so much potential to free himself—to *become* himself—apparent to us here now as an individual human being, but left to his own devices—very much of an ethereal prisoner stuck in the confines of some Pavlovian purgatory, at the mercy of his many present deficiencies, overwhelmed and overpowered by so many countless other types of beings with which he is here entangled in coexistence.

He has not yet come to develop the abilities through which to engage his own *will* and intervene. He can do little more than basically accept everything he here faces as real, true, and incontestable. But he may very well develop a conscience yet. He may very well develop a consensus of logic. He may very well someday come to develop the wits enough to intervene and declare his independence—to declare himself a sovereign individual human being amongst all these other beings—to declare himself a free will.

But as of yet, he offers no such remarkable signs of independence to speak of...

Birth of the Conscience

Out of the midst of that raging storm that is the constant and conflicted evolution of the will of a child—where emotions, sights and sounds, phantom engagements, and fits and tantrums are all being strewn about—something else is brewing—something else is percolating, burgeoning, becoming...his very own identity and self-awareness, his very own personal cares and concerns, and indeed—his very own conscience.

He gradually here and suddenly there begins to show remarkable signs of persona—of certain unique qualities, attributes, and characteristics—and of some basic inclinations to think and learn, and favor certain talents and interests.

Here and there, in certain instances, he even begins to exude stints of some apparent volition and perhaps a little pseudo-logic. He certainly exudes curiosity, and he most assuredly is intrigued—enough to provide all adults involved with as much interest and intrigue as they are willing to commit to engage.

Indeed, to come to know and realize his very own genuine personal cares and concerns—those behaviors, ideas, and interests which he will eventually come to know as his very own independent *rights*—such will in fact be his very own sovereign responsibility. Such will also be a-many-varied complex process of development, inevitably wrought with many challenges, from all apparent directions.

He will be bombarded by the interpretations and opinions of others, and he will have to scrutinize many forms and varieties of information in order to decipher, interpret, and determine any some such logical truths, rights, facts, or fictions thereof. It should be expected that he should one day inevitably come to know his very own sovereign rights and always be aware of and accountable for his very own sovereign limitations, such that he should furthermore come to act and react as a sane, viable, mature, responsible, independent individual living in society with others.

Understand here though, make no bones about this—those who will be involved in the responsible care and concern for such a child's upbringing should only thereby willingly intend to encourage said child to achieve these fulfillments of sovereignty and independence as thoroughly and sufficiently about his own free will, as much as he proves to be so willing and able to endure on his own individual efforts. In so doing, he will only therefore—true to form, true to content, true to context, and true to meaning—become exemplary of very much indeed—sovereignty, independence, and *freedom*.

Thus, it is here where the birth of the conscience comes to occur—the birth of an individual's very own consensus of awareness and self-awareness—an intersection of within and without—indeed a consensus to emerge out of an individual's very own complex of apprehensive senses, culminating in the development of one's most apt and fit, one's most qualified and equipped, sense enough to handle just such heavy concepts as those such as the likes of freedom, rights, and truth—one's very own consensus of logic.

Let us also submit here then, without any pretense, presumption, or presupposition, that it is in fact through one's very own conscience and consensus of logic that one can, should, and must continue to inquire, dissect, examine, and scrutinize any and all some such information, prejudices, presumptions, or presuppositions, in order to further determine and articulate any truths, rights, facts, fictions, or any potential errors or violations which may in fact come to occur to one's attention as invalid, incorrect, false, fallacious, or otherwise in contempt of freedom, right, truth, or logic.

As any sane, viable, mature and independent individual very well knows, the self-defeating youth—when he does come to reach such a stage of development, where he does so otherwise insist to rebel in such ways, either explicitly or implicitly, in contempt of his very own consensus of logic—is only there really rebelling against *himself*, and in fact, against that which he so adamantly insists he already has attained—his *freedom*.

At this stage, he has indeed already begun to come into some semblance of self-awareness, but his sense and consensus of logic have not quite yet developed as much as he so adamantly believes they have. He has here in fact dropped anchor prematurely. He has here come to the stage of fooling himself, tricking himself, and even believing that he has proven logic itself and everyone else around him to be wrong.

Well good—at least he's showing some guts.

But as to what had so previously felt to be so imposed upon him as to seem so apparently incontestable, he has now instead come into the feeling of a new sense of empowerment—where he now feels able to offer doubt and contest, and even impose his very own preferences and decisions, and even often exercise them in such a seemingly instinctive manner that he assumes he has here sufficiently completed the task of achieving freedom.

But all too often, in his zeal, he fails to realize, or he simply refuses to entertain the possibility of realizing that so many of his decisions are still very much made at the behest of those same old physical wants, emotional urges, and mythical desires. What he has yet to comprehend and determine as right about his decisions remains to be further resolved through sustained efforts of logic.

So what the adolescent really needs here is a mirror. And not just a mirror to be concerned with mere appearances—but rather a mirror to look through, behind, beyond, and more deeply into the comprehensive guts of what he only here simply *apprehends*—what he only merely sees, hears, feels, believes, and so forth—such that he may in fact come to eventually comprehend and appreciate the deeper, more genuine and more profound implications behind all of these waves of apprehensive information he has here been constantly contending with.

But even more thoroughly, more importantly, and more precisely, he should now come to appreciate the very profound magnitude of the realization that the very logical interpretations of all these physical sensations, emotional feelings, and mythical beliefs will be very much in fact, after all, his very own sovereign responsibility—for which the individual right there in the mirror must ultimately be accountable to achieve.

No one else can rightly do this for him. This life he is living is, after all, his very own, and he will have to come to terms with this.

Again, while each individual is most assuredly not born free, each is at least born with a brain and some potential—and each is at least therefore apt enough to come to exert the individual efforts necessary to develop and fulfill such a unique plethora of tremendously profound sensory, subconscious, and conscious potential.

Hence—with careful, persistent, and relentless effort, and with a strong will and vigorous spirit, and with tenacious intellect—in rightful denunciation of laziness and ignorance—each individual here thus can, may, and should indeed at least become apt and astute enough to stand representative of, in fact—a *free will*.

A strong will, a vigorous spirit, and a tenacious intellect will always lend much to advance any child's sovereignty and independence. So anywhere an adult is willing to foster and encourage a child's abilities to become such a sovereign and independent individual human being, an adult is there indeed doing right by that child.

Where any adult would otherwise stand, either explicitly or implicitly, to impede, discourage, deny, or deprive a child of a course pursuant to the child's independence, we know such a detractor or oppressor to be one made of either tyranny or truancy—or both. And as such, tyranny or truancy will become fostered and encouraged within the child, instead of freedom and independence—and the child's progress towards maturity will only there become further stagnated.

The upbringing of a child is therefore not a task to be left into the hands of tyranny or truancy.

It is here instead the collective responsibility of the parents and other family members, the teachers, and all other mentors familiar with the child, as well as indeed the child himself, to come to understand the process of maturity as a process of *learning*—and not as just a simple process of getting older, or as some mundane chore which has been imposed upon them all, to simply brush out of the way.

Moreover, the process of education should not be construed as just some mundane task by which to simply memorize information and then just regurgitate the information back out to get a good grade and pass a class, and then to graduate, and then to be done with all of this stuff. More than just a simple process of collecting and spilling bits and pieces of information, education should be intended to foster and encourage the development of the child's mind and conscience, to develop the intellect and self-awareness, to develop cognitive skills and functions, to develop comprehension and a comprehensive consensus of logic, to develop responsibility and accountability, to mature physically, emotionally, mythically, and logically, and to further mature, improve, and evolve as a sovereign and comprehensive individual—and to become such a rightly creative, responsible, accountable, sovereign and independent individual human being.

If truancy is instead fostered within the child early, the child will only develop a habit of truancy and will only come to regard his education as merely some dreadful burden which has been imposed upon him. His intellectual development and the development of his sense and consensus of logic will be stunted. He will remain immature. He will remain truant. He will remain stuck as a mere prisoner to physical wants, emotional urges, and mythical desires. He will live in the delusional belief that he is free—when, in reality—he is actually quite a long way from the efforts necessary to earn any such rightful claim to be an example of any such *freedom*.

Ultimately, as the evolution of the will of a child progresses—he can, may, and very well *should* instead be coming to make sense of so much about his own experiences and all that he comes to encounter within himself and about his environment and the nature of reality in which he here exists—through all the apprehensive physical activities, through all the emotional reactions, through all the mythical engagements—through the dubious and implausible depths of the subconscious, through the many burgeoning abstract and intricate surges and strands and developments and ideas—to so come to intervene with this experience of human being—to make sense of and articulate so many rights and truths about these various experiences, through all that will eventually rise to become—the tenacious, the resilient, and the strangely-sophisticated—the tremendous, the complex, and the comprehensive consensus of logic—ready to come up and come about—like the eye of the arthropod—so too, *the birth of the conscience.*

The conscience—mankind's modus operandi of identity, improvement, and independence. Linguistically speaking—"con-science"—quite literally, "with-science"—or rather, "with the wits of knowing"—or perhaps, more precisely—"*with-logic*". To be *with logic* is to be in one's right state of mind. It is where we become aware of self, aware of our experience of existence and of our involvement with other beings, aware of our physical, emotional, and mythical senses, and the nature of these senses.

It is where one must also become aware of the sovereignty of oneself—where the individual here becomes aware of himself as a sovereign individual human being, in societal communication with other individuals.

The individual here becomes aware of himself as an individual—and thus, he here unlocks his potential to intend to create any further or future causes, purposes, and objectives to which, for which, through which, and about which he has in fact developed such a conscience and consensus of logic in order to fulfill.

It is here then, with the burgeoning and ongoing development of the conscience that the individual can truly be said to be beginning to realize the triumph of the development of his consensus of logic—where he has now developed the faculties through which to intervene upon the unjust tyrannies and truancies of so many wants, whims, wishes, urges, and desires—to now become capable of dissecting and examining the information received through his sensory experience, to further inquire and investigate—so as to then come to determine and articulate so many truths and rights, so as to rightly conduct so many forward causes, purposes, and objectives in the interests of freedom and independence.

From the very onset of birth, as the individual progresses through so many various phases of sensory experience, through so many various stages of sensory development, he thus becomes further consciously aware of so many plural, diverse, and kinetic sights, sounds, smells, tastes, touches, feelings, beliefs, etc. He becomes capable of enduring the process of maturity, through the variable progressions of sensory experience and awareness of the physical, the emotional, the mythical, and ultimately—the logical.

These need not necessarily be understood to occur in such a rigid linear progression, but the more apprehensive senses do very much indeed tend to occur and develop first—and for that—they are thus only more simplistic. These apprehensive senses are only much more basic and immediate and developed only to serve the more basic and immediate reactive functions of life. They develop and plateau earlier in the individual's development. They lend only to very basic and simplistic modes and means of survival.

But our compound and *comprehensive* consensus of logic—a vast and variable, pluralistic and kinetic conjunction and convention of the conscience—a *common sense* in and of its own right—also very much of a bringing together of other senses—of inner sights and sounds—as *sound logic*—as being composed of so many abstract and complex faculties, functions, and operations—does so indeed develop, like so many wisdom teeth—not as an afterthought, or a suffix, but rather more slow and steady—as the slow *trane* of logic—as the course of maturity—as the course of contemplation, consideration, comprehension, and creativity—requisite of so much more persistence and resilience and tenacity and courage and depth and profundity and attention and focus and *effort*.

Indeed, our *mythos*—our mythical senses and faculties—compose a bit of a compound in and of itself—but a simple compound—an apprehensive compound—indeed, so much of a theater of apparitional sensations and emotions, where any and all mythical engagements and scenarios—all of an individual's wants, whims, wishes, urges, feelings, and desires are welcomed to be personified, and so often deified and entertained.

Indeed here, anything may appear possible and plausible. And why wouldn't it? Combine sights and sounds and charge them with emotions, and then simply subordinate logic to the position of a mere servant—and there you have a recipe for all kinds of wild results.

Physical sensations, emotional feelings, and mythical beliefs only become but a tyrant and a dictator if so appointed to the position of a judge. They are neither qualified nor equipped to determine or articulate any some such truths or rights at all. By contrast, our consensus of logic comes to represent an emancipation from the many potential unjust tyrannies of physical, emotional, and mythical impulses. Logic instead comes to act as very much of a rightful governor and judge of truth, right, and law.

As sane, viable, mature and independent human beings, we make right-minded decisions with logic. We then become capable of enjoying the fruits of our very own right-minded logical decisions out here in the real world, amongst the plural, diverse, and kinetic individual human beings with whom we so come to encounter and interact with and relate to in society.

We only effectively *rehearse* the scenarios that lead to these logical decisions within our mythos. Humanity and individuals of a free society do not care to see any of those violent and offensive rehearsals enacted out here in the real world, at the very real expense of human lives, human dignity, human rights, and human freedom—in blatant contempt, contradiction, and disregard for the true meaning, value, and spirit of freedom and independence.

Here then comes the triumph of the birth of the conscience.

Quite literally an evolutionary development.

The individual human being indeed here evolves a conscience as a necessary arbitration upon all the chaotic and irrational affairs of his physical sensations, emotional feelings, and mythical beliefs—so as to act as a court-of-appeal in which, through which, and by which to instill some semblance of truth, *rights*, and laws—through which to conduct and manage the information and affairs brought upon by these sensations, feelings, beliefs, thoughts, and behaviors in a rightfully logical and independent manner, as such a sovereign individual human being—with respect towards the value of individual sovereignty in society.

Through these evolutionary developments of the conscience and consensus of logic, each individual thus becomes apt, able, and mature enough to stand as *Representative* of each's very own rightly sovereign and independent will.

To reiterate, freedom is not something an individual human being can be rightly said to possess pre-consciously. Human beings cannot rightly be said to be "born free". Freedom is rather rightly indeed a logical intellectual development—and moreover, in fact—an evolutionary development from within the human intellect.

Freedom is a very highly sophisticated concept—and as such, it is one not rightly decided with physical sensations, emotional feelings, or mythical beliefs. Freedom is only rather rightly known by exercises of logic. Hence, we cannot allow freedom to be a concept given to the unfit and unqualified hands of any of the mere physical, emotional, or mythical senses.

Where any individual believes to be acting in the interests of freedom by simply *doing what he wants,* without any further ado—at the mercy of his own physical, emotional, or mythical impulses—in blatant contempt of logic—in blatant disregard for the sovereignty of others, as well as his own—he is there only acting in the interests of tyranny or truancy, in contempt and contradiction of the very true logical meaning of freedom.

Evolution of Logic

NOW THEN—THE INDIVIDUAL HAS about himself a *conscience*. Thus, he now also has developed about himself a consensus of logic—in which, by which, and through which to come to intervene upon his complex individual experience of being—and to further hold court over his physical, emotional, and mythical senses.

So now he can, should, and indeed *will*—if he be so astute enough to realize that this now is the very presentation of the course of freedom and independence—begin to truly appreciate the ongoing maturation of his own conscience—where he now indeed must begin to become so qualified and equipped enough to account for himself and his very own sovereign ownership of rights—enough to determine and articulate his very own genuine, personal, and independent cares and concerns, and indeed his very own independent thoughts, ideas, interests, tastes, tendencies, preferences, purposes, and causes.

Such a consensus of logic now must become a court-of-appeal in which, by which, and through which to assess, determine, articulate, and adjudicate any truth or rights at all. No other sense is either qualified or equipped enough to serve this very purpose. Neither sight nor sound, neither emotion nor belief, should be appointed to perform such a heavy task.

Physical sensations do not, on their own account, justify or validate any some such truth or right at all. Sights, sounds, smells, tastes, touches, etc. are only apprehensive experiences of sensations—and as such, these become no more than mere presumptuous perceptions on their own apprehensive account alone. Thus, these provide no such *comprehension* of any knowledge of truth or right at all.

Emotional feelings do not, on their own account, justify or validate any some such truth or right at all. Feelings are only apprehensive experiences of emotions—and as such, these become no more than mere presumptuous perceptions on their own apprehensive account alone. Thus, these also provide no such comprehension of any knowledge of truth or right at all.

Mythical beliefs also do not, on their own account, justify or validate any some such truth or right at all. Beliefs are only apprehensive experiences of myths, in which physical wants and emotional urges become manifested and person-ified—and so often *deified*—and entertained through ap-paritional mythical scenarios within an effectively subcon-scious arena—portrayed through the imagination to varying degrees of desire—an image, a story, a sound, a statement, a wish, a hope, a fear—and as such, these mythical engage-ments become no more than mere presumptuous percep-tions on their own apprehensive account alone. Therefore, these also provide no such comprehension of any knowledge of truth or right at all.

Logical concepts are thus conceived to intervene and ad-judicate the affairs of the physical, emotional, and mythical experiences of human being—to thus rightly serve the very purpose of ascertaining knowledge and *comprehension* of truth, right, laws, and the value of freedom.

What physical sensations, emotional feelings, and mythical beliefs *lack*, in and of themselves, is a true discretionary court of appeal by which to justify and validate knowledge of any such truth or right at all. For if *any* physical sensation, emotional feeling, or mythical belief is awarded validity of truth and right on its own apprehensive account alone, then *all* physical sensations, emotional feelings, and mythical beliefs must therefore be awarded validity of truth and right as well. Knowledge of truth and right would in fact there lose all meaning whatsoever. Physical sensations, emotional feelings, and mythical beliefs would simply run amuck—in a perpetual state of war and violence, each claiming to own absolute supremacy of truth and right, without any regard for further appeal to such a court and consensus of logic.

Without appeal to such a court of logic, we would only revert back to the ways of infants or wild animals, as prisoners to a chaotic war of physical, emotional, and mythical impulses—or much worse.

Our physical, emotional, and mythical senses are notorious for tricking us, fooling us, and leading us astray. It is only rightly *with logic* that we here come to right the ownership of true knowledge and make sense of our experiences of existence.

We are not yet so appreciative of the evolution of our faculties of logic, of the evolution of our consensus of logic, of the evolution of the very logical concepts of *truth, right,* and *law*. Nor are we so appreciative of the evolution of the conscience—nor of the evolution of the phenomenon of consciousness itself. How easily we simply take these for granted and presume to believe that truth, right, and knowledge were ever so complete and *absolutely* given, impervious to change, and somehow resolved long before our birth.

But our purposes are forward, not backwards.

It is not productive for us to demand to stand pat and chastise the very notion of evolution, or *change*, in general. The notion of truth and right evolving over time may have seemed unsettling to ancient people of the past, since they had always been told that truth and right were absolute, impervious to doubt, impervious to change, and divinely given—*or else!* But the evolution of logic has allowed us to gain a clearer perspective as to the kinetic nature of knowledge and existence.

How easily though we became so obsessed with the presumption that our knowledge comes to us as if it falls out of the sky—so totally and completely pre-packaged and categorically absolute. As if our knowledge has not always been so prone to persistently change, develop, improve, and evolve. As if we are not always apt to improve our comprehension of knowledge and comprehension of what is right and true about the very nature of our existence. As if we are not so apt to further evolve.

But haven't this and that—these and those—our very conscience and consensus of logic—indeed occurred as evolutionary developments? Did we not in fact develop this conscience and these faculties of logic in order to serve this very purpose of determining truth and right at all? Did we not in fact *need* to develop this conscience and these faculties of logic in order to, first—survive, and then—to further come to gain knowledge, create our advancements and improvements, and declare our independence from the ways of the wild—to bring order to the court of such physical, emotional, and mythical chaos—and to contract such logical social agreements with other individual human beings?

Didn't our very own efforts and exercises of our very own human brains in fact cause us humans to effect change and improve and evolve our awareness and understanding of our knowledge of the nature of our realm of existence?

We have only relatively recently, with respect to the evolution of mankind, become aware of ourselves as a creative species—as a species capable of creating and furthering knowledge—as a species capable of causing and creating improvements—as a species capable of *causing* ourselves to effect changes and improvements, through the collaborative and contributive efforts of so many individuals over the course of time—toward the improvement of each and every individual human being, capable of causing oneself to improve, mature, and evolve—towards the appreciation of each's own sovereign potential.

We have only relatively recently become aware of our minds' intrinsic involvement in the experience of what we have only far too long presumed to be an absolute and pre-determined reality. We have only relatively recently become aware of the profound nature of consciousness and of the individual's intrinsic and necessary involvement in one's own experience of existence and one's own knowledge of being.

But indeed, a human being is evident as an individual before he really develops a conscience. A conscience certainly does not exist without a sole, individual constitution of human being from which it develops. Upon birth, the individual indeed becomes evident to us as a sole constitution of human being—but he certainly does not there yet provide us with sufficient evidence of a conscience. For what the individual there has yet left to develop in terms of a conscience, or what he has yet left to develop in terms of any some such sovereignty, independence, or *freedom* at all—is, at birth—still yet unremarkable, if not altogether null and void.

The individual's conscience does thus very much indeed come to occur as an evolutionary development.

Furthermore—if to indulge ourselves in somewhat of a metaphor about this: consider that the development of the conscience comes to occur through a-many-varied complex process of subconscious *training*—in order to effectively become "hired" by one's very own distinct and tumultuous *will*—to thus come about and serve as governor, manager, executor, and conductor of so many chaotic affairs about one's very own personal, plural, diverse, and kinetic *business* of human being.

The *Conscience*—to now stand to act and react as the sole accountable *Representative, Governor,* and *Executor* of each one's very own distinct individual constitution of human being.

Conscience—now as governor, representative, and executor of an individual's very own sovereign and independent will—to now make sense of and conduct so many plural, diverse, kinetic, and apprehensive experiences of physical sensations, emotional feelings, mythical beliefs, and so forth. And now also to serve as such a court-of-appeal in which, through which, and by which to so engage with one's faculties of logic, in order to rightly and logically adjudicate rights and establish ownership of these rights, in communicative society with other rightly sovereign and independent individual human beings.

Truly, the individual human being initially begins his development as that of very much only an *effector*—primarily only reacting in response to so many plural, diverse, and kinetic apprehensive stimuli from within, without, and about his personal realm of experience. But then, he eventually matures enough to become *aware* of himself as an effector. Thus, he develops a conscience and consensus of logic—through which logical concepts are contracted and developed to consciously intervene and come to instill some semblance of truth, right, law, freedom, liberty, equality, and justice, and so forth.

Such evolutionary processes and developments have indeed only very much come to occur as a result of so many collaborative and contributive efforts of so many plural, diverse, and kinetic individual human beings over the entire course of the evolution of the species, over a relatively exhaustive and immense period of time, through all the hominid types, culminating in the present specific type—Homo sapiens sapiens.

Being the plural, diverse, and kinetic species we are—each individual, being of such a unique and distinct conscience and consensus of logic, and so thus apt and fit enough to stand as *Representative* of each one's very own free will—the value of freedom should now indeed begin to become quite clear.

The maturation of the conscience here then becomes evident as the very true declaration of an individual's independence. The individual at least now becomes aware of his potential *for* freedom. He at least now becomes aware of himself as capable of causing creative results. He thus becomes aware of himself as a progenitor.

Initially only an effector, then a progenitor, the individual thus becomes quite literally—a creator.

We should take note here and concur with the notion of how easily a prehistoric human could have presumed the early stages of the birth of the conscience to be some other voice—some up there, out there voice—amongst the stars—some celestial voice calling to him from elsewhere.

Having not yet developed the faculties of logic enough to exercise discretion, the individual would have there failed to realize that this shadowy echo of a "voice" *in his head* was in fact his very own conscience. Like an animal seeing its reflection in a pool of water for the first time, he would have failed the test of recognizing himself in this audio "reflection". He would have been confused and perhaps afraid. He would have lacked the logical development through which to intervene and understand the language of myth and metaphor, and he would have very easily mistaken this ghostly development as some universal creator of everything, up there, out there, outside of himself.

The individual would have then there failed to recognize this apparitional manifestation as the mythical projection of the *birth of the conscience* towards the human-being-in-general as becoming a creative individual—as becoming a *maker* of things—as becoming a *creative* species, as well as the mythical projection of some personified ideals of the human form.

The individual would have thus also failed to recognize this as the projection and mythical personification of one's own notions of one's *ideal* selves—tomorrow, future, better, more mature versions of oneself toward which one is inclined to aspire and orient and effort oneself to become and fulfill through the progressive stages of maturation.

The individual would have there failed to recognize that this is all happening to occur within himself, from himself, to himself, and about himself—as indeed, the penultimate rite of passage amongst all individual human beings—where each develops a conscience and comes to recognize oneself as a progenitor—as a *creator*—as a conscious and creative individual, capable of creating thoughts and forward causes, purposes, interests, and endeavors—and further, artifacts and tools and *things* with which to improve and better one's life, one's existence, one's self, and one's society.

The individual human being here comes to the stage of now effectively becoming representative of a *free* will. What further causes, purposes, interests, and endeavors he will now effectively come to create, and eventually intend to fulfill—these will always be his very own sovereign responsibility, and these should always be realized to occur on his very own sovereign account.

All that the individual will come to interpret as true and right about the various experiences of his physical sensations, emotional feelings, and mythical beliefs, he is now responsible for coming to determine and articulate through his very own conscience and consensus of logic.

As stated—physical sensations, emotional feelings, and mythical beliefs do not, on their own account, have the qualifications to comprehend and ascertain knowledge of truth or right. In spite of logic, these faculties remain simple reactions of only so much of an effector—unable to move beyond its own apprehensive experience and come to a more comprehensive awareness of the more profound nature of all of these sensory experiences.

The individual here then necessarily creates for himself a mirror—a *conscience*—where he now not only becomes aware of himself as a simple *effector* reacting to all these sensory experiences, but he now also becomes fit enough to become aware of himself as a sovereign experience of human being—and herewith the development of his consensus of logic—becomes a court-of-appeal in which, through which, and by which to manage, to govern, and to conduct the affairs of so many plural, diverse, and kinetic experiences in order to establish certain truths, rights, and laws about these experiences—and to further come to contractualize certain social agreements with other individual human beings.

An individual's conscience need not become such a tyrant and impose commands upon him. His emotions and beliefs do quite a bit enough of that already.

The individual instead develops such a conscience, in fact, to free himself from just such tyrannical commands. No longer then is he held as such a prisoner or a slave to the irrational demands of his physical wants, emotional urges, and mythical desires. The individual himself now becomes the sovereign arbitrator, capable of warding off the many forms of tyranny and truancy and creating rightful courses of sovereignty.

Here then the value of freedom comes right up to the fore again. Further proof of the necessity of the conscience.

Human beings need such a court-of-appeal in which, through which, and by which to ascertain truths and establish certain laws in order to ensure freedom and to protect the sovereignty of human *rights*, so that tyranny and truancy may not overpower freedom and overtake the sovereignty of the individual—within oneself, or within any further context of society in which one here so comes to live.

Society

(The Consequence of Others)

AMONG THE MYRIAD CIRCUMSTANCES into which we are born, none is there more immediate and impending than the consequence that is other humans. For all that an individual will come to experience, for all that one will endeavor to pursue and all that one will intend to achieve—such will, at least to some extent, persistently involve and be affected by other humans.

Society is the consequence that—where there is one human being, there most assuredly is another. And where there is another—there are indeed many others. At almost every turn, there are always going to be other human beings around to contend with.

And so it is here then, in this crowded theater—*in the company of others*—where an individual's sense of freedom comes to be so persistently provoked and so pervasively challenged.

Somehow, somewhere—amongst all these others—an individual is going to have to find ways to fulfill one's own existence and make for oneself a genuine and meaningful course of life—a genuine and meaningful course of sovereign and independent identity, interests, ideas, values, behaviors, tastes, tendencies, preferences, property—and further *rights*.

Somehow, somewhere—in this tangled mess—an individual is going to have to find ways to maintain ownership of one's own being and one's own sovereign rights, and sustain a genuine and independent relationship with all the phenomenal occurrences that one comes to encounter here in this experience of existence—lest one be so constantly consumed and devoured and overpowered by some form of tyranny imposed upon us by some other individual or group of individuals.

The very real and true value of freedom thus here proves to be explicit.

It is here where an individual must necessarily and rightly come to declare one's *own* independence as a sovereign individual human being. It is here where an individual must necessarily and rightly come to distinguish between one's *own* existence and the existence of others—distinguish between one's *own* being and other beings—distinguish between one's own sovereign *experience* of human being and the sovereign experiences of other individuals.

The distinction of *ownership* here now becomes imperative.

It is here where an individual must always necessarily and rightly come to distinguish between what is *mine* and what is *not mine*—distinguish between my life and the lives of other individuals—distinguish between my body and other bodies—between my identity and not-my-identity—between my interests and not-my-interests—between my ideas and not-my-ideas—between my values and not-my-values—between my property and not-my-property...between my rights and not-my-rights—indeed, between my rights and the rights of others.

The question of rights and the question of freedom of rights then here becomes a matter of, first—asserting the sovereignty of the individual human being—of articulating the individual's sovereign ownership of rights—and of distinguishing between one individual's sovereign ownership of rights and another's.

So then, anywhere that two or more individuals do so come to convene to form a society, the underlying question which begs to be addressed between them is: how should these individuals go about engaging, interacting, communicating, and conducting themselves *rightly*—here in the company of others?

In other words: what is the right condition, manner, or *value*—in which, by which, and through which, such individuals are here to so rightly, justly—and further, *logically*—intend to engage, interact, communicate, and address one another in such a right and just society?

More to the point—what is the value here of greatest mutual regard?

The correct answer is *freedom*. The social condition, manner, and value in which individuals are rightly and justly realized and recognized as the very fundamental and elemental *beings*—of which, for which, by which, and about which, any given context of human society here ever comes to be formed or further known at all.

The individual human being is the very elemental component—the very fundamental sovereignty—of which any society or social contract is here, in fact, ever rightly and logically composed at all.

If we are ever even a society at all, then we are indeed only a society of *individuals*—a society of individual human beings.

Any society is only ever the individuals who constitute that particular society. A *society* has no such brain or mouth of its own from which to speak of "itself" or its own interests.

Individuals do.

And whatsoever is spoken of in the name of society, or in the interests of a society, is only ever spoken of by the mouths of individual human beings, alone or in concert.

And whatsoever is written about any society, or further written about the interests of any society, is only ever written by the hands of individual human beings.

All who are involved here or elsewhere in any discussion of society, or in any discussion about the interests of a society, are involved only as individuals—each of only rightly his or her very own sovereign and independent account. No one individual, nor any particular group of individuals rightly represents a singular and absolute set of values or interests for any "entire society" as a whole.

It is only by the most arrogant and egregious examples of tyranny that any individual or group of individuals ever pretends to own or speak for the experiences, interests, values, or further rights, of *all* individuals.

Each individual is here only rightly capable of conveying perspectives from the viewpoint of his or her very own sovereign and independent experience of human being. None can ever rightly claim to own the experience of any other being but one's own. All that one knows about other beings, one knows only from the vantage point of one's very own sovereign account.

One cannot rightly occupy the experience of another being or pretend to own the experience of another being. Each individual human being is here only ever rightly a sovereign and independent *version* of human experience.

Each individual here then only rightly comes to the table of society as representative of one's very own sole, sovereign, and independent experience of human being.

One does not rightly override, invade, or otherwise encroach upon the sovereignty of another individual—as the sovereignty of another individual exists outside the ownership of one's own sovereign being. The sovereignty of another individual exists outside the rightful and logical scope of one's own sovereign ownership of freedom or rights.

Any laws made then to govern the various engagements, interactions, and communications which may come to occur between the individuals involved in any given context of human society, therefore, can only be made rightly and justly with respect to the *sovereignty of the individual* as the very right and just premise. The sovereignty of the individual is indeed paramount to the formulation of the laws of any right and just social contract—as societies and social contracts cannot possibly even exist without individual human beings here and present to form and contract them.

We are only rightly and logically *responsible* for this. In other words, we are in fact the very individuals who are rightly responsible for creating any such providence of freedom—and for creating any such society made in the interests of freedom, and for creating such right and just laws made to uphold and appreciate the very right and just value of the sovereignty of individuals and to always repel the many insatiable efforts of tyranny.

If the laws of a society are to be made rightly and justly—which is to say, made in the interests of freedom—then such *laws* are only rightly and justly made *with logic*, by individual citizens, for individual citizens, and about individual citizens—to protect and serve the sovereignty and independence of each and every individual citizen.

To be sure—in any form or context of society—conflicts of interest between individuals will indeed inevitably happen to occur. But that these conflicts can or will ever even happen to occur at all is only proof of the very fact that there are indeed such different and distinct individuals, with such different and distinct identities, interests, ideas, and values, here and present to cause any some such conflicts to occur in the first place.

And where such conflicts are indeed so prone to occur, it thus becomes even more necessary to contractualize certain agreements upon which to uphold the very rightful and logical respect and appreciation of the true value of freedom, with certain laws made to always ensure to protect the sovereignty of the individual citizen and to always repel against the many inclinations of tyranny—where individuals, alone or conspired together with others, in sheer spite and contempt of the true meaning and real value of freedom, intend to impose supremacy and dominance of their own particular prejudices and wage war against the sovereignty of other individuals.

It is worth reminding here that the long history of human civilization, or "civilized" society, was not made with any remarkable interest in the value of freedom or with any such respect for the sovereignty of individuals. The history of human society is a story rather made in the interests of those very same old inclinations of the wild. It is a story made of tyranny—of so many individuals and groups of individuals, driven by the obsession to impose supremacy and dominance of their particular wants, whims, wishes, urges, feelings, beliefs, and desires upon all other individuals—in sheer spite and contempt of the mere mention of the notion of the value of freedom.

It is naive to presume that civilization or civilized society was ever made or founded upon any sort of innocent, peaceful, or noble intentions.

The history of civilized society certainly suggests otherwise.

The history of civilized society suggests that civilization was indeed forged and founded upon those very same old archaic inclinations of tyranny—of the manipulation, exploitation, enslavement, subordination, and domestication of other human beings.

The history of civilized society has evidenced very little to no regard at all for the value of freedom and the sovereignty of individual human beings. Any interest expressed towards the value of freedom throughout history has always been overruled and demolished by the heavy fists of authoritarianism—through all the tyrannies of the ancient world, under the spell of the atrocities of the dark and middle ages, up to and including the variations that continue to persist today, in various contexts and capacities and to varying degrees of authoritarian and totalitarian rule.

Authoritarianism has always looked upon other human beings as mere slaves, servants, peasants, patrons, pawns, prisoners, or prey. To the powers of absolute authority, the individual human being is, at best, little more than a menial dupe—a mere resource to be exploited. At worst, the individual is treated as an object of torture.

Authoritarianism instills fear, imposes its might, and assumes control of ownership over the individual. Authoritarianism dictates people's identities, interests, ideas, values, and purposes to them. It not only discourages individuals from determining their own sovereign purposes, it often outright prevents them from owning the ability to even make such sovereign determinations at all. To the powers of tyranny, the individual is not viewed as an owner of *anything*—let alone as an owner of oneself, one's own unique identity, interests, ideas, values, any such parcel of land, or any semblance of further rights whatsoever.

It is only relatively recently, within just the past few hundred years, that human beings have even begun the process of coming to collectively understand, appreciate, and further educate the very logical, right, and true value of freedom and to resist the many tyrannies of totalitarianism, authoritarianism, fascism, and dictatorships of every sort.

For thousands of years, authoritarian regimes have held a blanket over the entire population of humanity and suffocated the progress of freedom.

To this day, by and large—they still do.

Whether the modern regimes are simply ignorant to the true meaning of freedom or whether their appetite for power is intentionally malicious towards the value of freedom altogether really makes no difference—in either case, tyranny is still made in contempt of freedom and logic.

The engagements, interactions, and relationships between human beings have always been polluted by tyranny. It has always tended to occur, and continues to occur, by those same old impulsive ways of the wild—individuals and groups of individuals seek to impose supremacy and dominance of some particular cultured prejudices over others and dictate to other individuals what particular identity traits, interests, ideas, values, or beliefs that they shall revere as supreme and right, and which ones that they shall condemn as inferior and wrong—those towards which tyranny commands them to vilify, condemn, and destroy.

But who is so rightly endowed to judge the interests of all? Who but the individual himself or herself can possibly come to know the sovereign rights about his or her very own being? Who but the individual himself or herself can possibly own the sovereign experience of being through which to come to recognize, realize, and know the very identity, interests, ideas, values, behaviors, tastes, tendencies, and preferences that one will come to identify as rightfully one's own?

What traits, what values, and what interests the individual will come to determine to be *right*—those which one will come to know as one's very own—can only rightly and logically be one's very own sovereign responsibility to determine.

No other individual, nor any particular group of individuals, of any particular context or capacity, rightly subverts the sovereignty of the individual or denies an individual his or her sovereign and independent *ownership* of rights.

Each individual here—being so rightly representative of such a sovereign and independent ownership of rights—of such unique identity, interests, ideas, and values of one's own—is thus right to endeavor to pursue and fulfill one's very own sovereign and independent courses of interest, to the best of one's very own sovereign and independent abilities.

Where one is acting in the interests of freedom—within one's own sovereign ownership of rights—one is there most certainly acting within one's logical right to proceed upon such sovereign and independent courses of interest.

The value of freedom still has a long way to go to be realized and actualized. It certainly has not come to fruition. Nor has it yet become sufficiently understood. But it is indeed our very inherent responsibility to create the providence of freedom. The providence of freedom is neither naturally nor absolutely given—just as with any other knowledge. We humans create the providence of knowledge. So too, we must also create the providence of freedom.

To give to the appreciation of freedom, one need only do what is only rightly one's most principal and essential responsibility anyway—to live up to one's own fullest sovereign potential. To become a sovereign individual and to live a sovereign and independent life, as a sovereign representative of an individual experience of human being, to act in the interests of sovereignty and independence, and to thus act in the interests of freedom, one thereby inherently communicates a spirit of freedom to others.

Hence, the value of freedom is indeed mutually productive.

What purpose or what benefit could an individual otherwise possibly contribute to any such "greater good" if to only live a compromised version of one's life—a life of little to no freedom at all—as such an indentured servant or much worse? As a constant subordinate to others—as if this life you are living were not your own?

So to live toward one's own fullest sovereign potential, one there literally *appreciates* the value of freedom—within oneself, as well as *for* one's society in which one here participates.

If each component of a society, if each member of a society, if each individual human being within a society were living in such a condition of freedom, where each is expected and encouraged to live up to each's own fullest sovereign potential—then and only then could we rightly say that such a society would be truly living up to its own fullest sovereign potential.

To do otherwise—to live in contempt of freedom, or to live in a state of compromised or diminished freedom—would only serve to compromise not only the sovereignty of the individual, but also compromise the greater sovereignty of the society itself. To do so would only serve to allow tyranny and truancy to expand and persist to morph the society into a self-devouring Leviathianic beast.

So, either one rightly lives up to the true meaning of sovereignty and independence and forwards the progress and appreciation of the value of freedom for one and all, or one simply enables tyranny and truancy to thrive and threaten to run the species into a state of self-devouring oblivion.

The assembly of society and the contract of law must therefore only rightly and logically be made in the interests of freedom—to uphold and appreciate the imperative and essential value of the sovereignty of each and every individual.

Freedom is our first right. It is our quintessential right. Thus, it should be the principal and paramount interest and concern of any such right and just logical government.

There is no social interest of greater value and importance than freedom. Freedom covers the entirety of the population of a society—as it pertains to everyone, to each and every individual citizen. No particular cult or faction can outnumber the population that freedom covers. No matter how strong or vicious or malicious, or no matter how loud or large in number, no group can outnumber the coverage of freedom. The value of freedom is inclusive to literally one-hundred percent of the population.

Freedom is in fact independence from the many tyrannies that authoritarian regimes, dictatorships, cults, factions, and so forth come to impose upon humanity.

But tyranny is indeed pervasive and persistent.

Rights vs. Violations

TYRANNY MANIFESTS ITSELF IN many forms. The murderer, the rapist, the assailant—the thief, the arsonist, the extortionist—the despot, the terrorist, the bigot...

What they all have in common is that they all impose the same archetypical offense.

Each, in some particular form, imposes ownership, dictatorship, or absolute authority over the sovereignty and sovereign rights of other individuals.

Each is engaging in some variation of violation of freedom. Each is engaging in some form of invasion of sovereignty and subversion of the meaning of sovereignty. Each is engaging in some type of breach of ownership.

To violate right is to violate freedom—to subvert the meaning of sovereignty, to invade the sovereignty of another individual, to act in breach of ownership, and to impose such ownership, dictatorship, or absolute authority over the sovereignty and sovereign rights of other individuals—in contempt of the very logical definition of one's very own sovereign ownership of rights.

Such is the archetypical *wrong*—the archetypical *violation of right*. It is where the archetypical violation of sovereignty comes to occur.

The murderer violates by way of imposing ownership, dictatorship, or absolute authority over the lives of his or her victims.

The rapist and the assailant violate by imposing ownership, dictatorship, or absolute authority over the bodies of their victims.

The thief, the arsonist, and the extortionist violate by imposing ownership, dictatorship, or absolute authority over the money, assets, or other personal property of their victims.

The terrorist violates by imposing ownership, dictatorship, or absolute authority over some combination of his or her victims' lives, bodies, property, and so forth. The terrorist is typically driven by a fervent allegiance to some cult of personality, bent on waging supremacy and dominance of itself and its kind over others not of its kind.

The despot violates by imposing ownership, dictatorship, or absolute authority over the liberties of his or her victims. The despot is essentially a tyrant who has come into a position of high power and authority. The despot assumes the position of absolute authoritarian and dictates to his or her victims what identity traits, what beliefs, what values, and what interests they will adopt and revere as the absolute and supreme "right" ones and which ones they will condemn as the absolute "wrong" ones, how they will act, what they will do and how they will do it and when they will do it, how they will speak, who they will speak to and who they will not speak to, what they will wear and what they will not wear, what they will eat and when they will eat it and what they will not eat, or some similar host of other totalitarian commands.

The bigot violates by imposing ownership, dictatorship, or absolute authority over the value of his or her victims' identity and interests. The bigot is the underling of the terrorist and the despot. The bigot vicariously shares in the power of the terrorist and the despot by subscribing to their pretense of a supreme and absolute authority over others. The bigot degrades and condemns individuals of different identity traits, interests, and values than its own, and it further attempts to exclude those other individuals from owning certain human rights or participating in certain civil liberties. Or the bigot even further means to dismiss or deny the very value of other individuals' existence altogether.

These are the primary archetypes of tyranny. These are just some of the many faces of the violator and some of the many variations by which violations of freedom and violations of human rights come to occur.

In every case—violation of freedom, violation of sovereignty, violation of ownership, and violation of right are at play. It is only the type and severity of the violation that is different in each case.

In every case, it is a breach of ownership that occurs. Every form of the tyrant violates by assuming, imposing, or simply outright *taking* ownership over that which does not rightly belong to them or to their sovereign ownership of rights.

The murderer wrongly assumes ownership over someone else's sovereign life. The rapist wrongly assumes ownership over someone else's sovereign body. The thief wrongly assumes ownership over someone else's sovereign money or other property. The despot wrongly assumes ownership over someone else's sovereign liberties. The bigot wrongly assumes ownership over the values of someone else's sovereign interests or identity traits.

Every form of the tyrant wrongly assumes a position of supremacy and ownership over the values of other people and the sovereignty of other people's rights. The tyrant appoints itself to a position of *absolute authority* over others—to serve as judge, jury, and executioner over the "rights" of other individuals.

But one individual's experience of existence—one individual's being—one individual's sovereign will—one individual's sovereign ownership of a certain sovereign life, body, mind, property, values, interests—one individual's sovereign *rights*—do not rightly or logically belong to another individual or another individual's sovereign ownership of rights.

One individual does not logically or rightly own the sovereign will or represent the ownership of another individual's sovereign being or sovereign rights. One individual does not rightly overrule, invade, overtake, or own the sovereignty of another.

Sovereignty of the individual is mankind's quintessential right. And, indeed, subversion of this sovereignty is mankind's primal wrong—mankind's archetypical violation.

To violate the sovereignty of another individual is to violate right and commit wrong. To so invade, encroach upon, or otherwise attempt to impose such ownership, dictatorship, or absolute authority over the sovereignty and sovereign rights of another individual is the very premise of wrongful behavior. And such acts are, in fact, quite capable of being proven wrong by way of appeal to a court of logic.

The fundamental archetypical structure of all such violations of sovereignty is even further necessary to illustrate in order to formulate such rightful and logical contracts of law.

People will say they "know" that murder is indeed wrong. But yet very little is further offered with respect to providing the very simple logical explanation as to *why* such an act is, in fact—*wrong*. As if such a logical explanation were some sort of an insult or a distraction from the physical, emotional, or mythical perspective of the wrongness of murder—and not rather in fact, the *very law-gical* concept which itself comes to serve the very purpose of proving such an act to be wrong in the first place.

As if the physical, emotional, or mythical discomfort that arises from the awareness of an act such as murder were somehow more relevant and important to a discussion or contract of law and human rights than supplying a valid logical explanation as to the very archetypical nature of the wrongness of such an act?

But the physical, emotional, and mythical perspectives and reactions to murder do absolutely nothing on their own account to *prove* an act such as murder to be wrong. The difference between right and wrong is only rather rightly resolved through appeal to a court of logic.

What is logically right is the sovereignty of the individual—and what is wrong is the violation of this sovereignty, in all of its various manifestations, as those evidenced here in the act of murder, as well as those evidenced throughout the various other archetypical faces of tyranny.

What is right is freedom—and what is wrong is the violation of this freedom.

What is right is that which belongs to the sovereign ownership of the rightly free and independent individual—as representative of just such a rightly sovereign and independent ownership of rights—as an individual apart from, and independent of, other individuals and their own sovereign and independent ownerships of rights—as sovereign and independent individual human beings living towards the appreciable, and further, social interests of freedom.

Where one individual or group of individuals otherwise attempts to impose some form of tyranny and assume some form of ownership, dictatorship, or absolute authority over the *rights*—over the life, body, mind, values, interests, property, tastes, tendencies, preferences, and so forth, of another individual or over all other individuals—one is there only acting in violation of the sovereignty of ownership and the very logical meaning thereof.

One is there acting in contempt of freedom—in violation of freedom. One is there acting *against* freedom. And again, where one is acting in opposition to the value of freedom, one's actions cannot logically be awarded any rightful claim to be an act of freedom itself.

No individual can then ever rightly be said to be acting in the interests of freedom where he or she so comes to invade the sovereignty of another individual and pretend to assume any such ownership, dictatorship, or absolute authority over any other sane, viable individual's sovereign ownership of rights.

To do so, one is there only acting in breach, contempt, contradiction, and *violation* of sovereignty and the true logical meaning of freedom.

It is only by an act of brute force—and *not* by any such act of freedom—that one individual overtakes the sovereignty of another.

Taken here in the most extreme context—consider that the murderer cannot rightly claim it to be any act or exercise of freedom to murder another individual, since the murderer is only thereby assuming ownership over a life which does not logically or rightly belong to his or her sovereign ownership of freedom—or, to his or her sovereign ownership of rights.

Virtually all sane, viable individuals obviously would agree that the act of murder elicits reactions of emotional contempt, but we should come to further appreciate the greater importance of providing and comprehending the very logical explanation as to *why* such an act as murder is in fact—*wrong*. Why such an act is *not right*—and not an act of freedom.

It should be very basic and elementary to recognize the fact that the laws of a right and just society can only actually be made rightly and justly with *logic*. Logic is the rightful and literal root of *law*. With logic then, we come to ascertain and articulate the archetypical structure by which violations of rights come to occur.

How troubling it is then that the act of murder fits precisely into what the zealous seem to believe freedom means—since, after all, the murderer is simply only *doing what he wants* when he assumes such ownership over the life of his victim.

But let us be very clear about this—an individual is most certainly *not* acting in the interests of freedom when he or she comes to commit such a breach of ownership, in blatant contempt and disregard for the true logical meaning and very real value of the sovereignty of ownership, as exampled here in the most extreme among the many forms of tyranny, such as murder is, in addition to the many other forms.

Murder is not an act of freedom—murder is an act of anti-freedom. It is among the most extreme and severe forms of the acts of anti-freedom to pretend to assume ownership over a life which does not rightly or logically belong to your sovereign ownership of rights—a life which does not rightly or logically belong to your sovereign ownership of freedom.

By the same form of occurrence—rape, assault, robbery, terrorism, despotism, bigotry—none of these are acts of freedom. These are all acts of *anti-freedom*.

These are not acts exercised in the interests of freedom—they are instead acts committed *against* the interests of freedom. They are acts committed in contempt of the very value of freedom and the sovereignty of ownership.

What we have so often failed to comprehend is that acts of tyranny are not just acts committed as an insult against one particular individual or another, they are in fact committed against the very essence of the meaning of the concept of freedom at all—which is to say, they are acts committed against the very nature of even one's own sovereignty and independence. They are blatant contradictions of freedom. One cannot rightly be sovereign and independent *from* others if one is bound to others in such conditions of tyranny.

To impose an act of tyranny is to affect a pretense of absolute authority and to assume a pretense of absolute ownership over the rights and values of others. It is to affect the pretense of an ownership outside the bounds of the meaning of freedom and to affect the pretense of a "freedom" outside the bounds of one's ownership—an ownership which one does not rightly or logically have any such right to claim to own. It is inherently false, fallacious, and erroneous to claim such an ownership to which all other human beings are supposedly somehow just mere subordinates.

To be free means to be a sole, sovereign, and independent individual experience of (human) being. Freedom does not carry any sort of privelege to own, dictate, or invade the sovereignty of other individuals. It is no such rightful interpretation of the meaning of freedom to construe it as a license to move as some unstoppable blanket force, entitled to simply mow others down.

Thus, virtually all acts that occur as wrongs, crimes, or violations, occur as some form of breach of ownership of rights—in breach and violation of the true logical meaning of freedom. Where one simply overtakes and devours the sovereignty of another, one is there explicitly acting in blatant contempt and disregard for the true value of sovereignty and the true meaning of freedom.

What is provided here then as logically *right*, in terms of human behavior in society, begins upon the very intrinsic and imperative value of the sovereignty of the individual human being as the very fundamental and elemental premise upon which any such right and just laws are to be contracted. That each individual is rightly sovereign unto one's very own sovereign ownership of one's very own sovereign rights and one's very own sovereign limitations.

What is right is the sovereignty of the individual. What are an individual's rights are too many in number to count. Rights are those ideas, interests, values, traits, characteristics, properties etc. that an individual comes to know as *right* for oneself—as rightly one's own. Rights are for an individual oneself to come to determine through efforts of one's very own sovereign being.

Each is here then the only rightful owner of one's own sovereign values and interests.

What is wrong then is the violation of this sovereignty. What is wrong is that which occurs where an individual or group of individuals comes to impose supremacy and dominance of a particular prejudice over the sovereignty and sovereign rights of other individuals.

This notion of supremacy and superiority becomes even more emboldened and empowered in individuals when they are met in agreement with others of a common prejudice. The more populated a prejudice can make itself become, the more forceful its discriminative power against others of different identity, interests, and values becomes.

Sovereignty vs. Supremacy

(Freedom vs. Tyranny)

"*IF IT DOESN'T LOOK like me, act like me, or think like me—kill it!, imprison it!, enslave it!, or otherwise deny it freedom and rights!*"

Throughout the entire course of human history, such has been the nature of what we might call the war-cry of the supremacist. It is that primitive and archaic impulse and inclination of territorialistic supremacy—the provocation and promotion of the territorial and tyrannical attitude that *whatever is not me is my enemy*.

It is the manifestation of the physical want, emotional urge, and mythical desire to impose supremacy and dominance and condemn all others not of one's likeness—to believe one's particular cultivated identity, interests, and values to be the absolute, supreme, right, moral, and superior kind—and to condemn all those of different identities, interests, and values to be bad, wrong, immoral, inferior, or less than human.

It is here once again the same old archetypical act of imposing ownership, dictatorship, and absolute authority over the sovereignty and sovereign rights of other individuals. It is here once again that same old impulsive habit of tyranny rearing its ominous head. And it is here once more another form of truancy—as it is always much *easier* to condemn other individuals than it is to put forth the sovereign efforts necessary to resolve one's own insecurities.

The tyrannical impulse here imposes itself in such a way as to affect the pretense that there is only one supreme and absolute right way to live—whatever way the particular tyrant who proposed it says is the supreme and absolute right way to live.

The tyrannical view thus looks upon human beings and human nature as always having but one singular right way and many wrongs.

But it is a pretense which is ultimately only contrary to reality and the logic of freedom—since there are at least as many right ways to live as there are people.

There is indeed, however, one primary archetypical wrong—which is to assume such supremacy of one particular category of individual and to impose such ownership, dictatorship, or absolute authority over the sovereignty and sovereign rights of other individuals.

Tyranny perpetuates tyranny. To impose supremacy of one particular kind and to promote prejudice against other kinds is, by design, to contradict the very value of freedom and to enable the proliferation of tyranny. This only comes to serve to encourage human beings to devolve back towards the ways of the past—towards a condition of perpetual violence and war and constant vying for supremacy and dominance of a particular interest, value, type, category, cult, or kind of human being.

Tyranny is the primary reason we had to develop a sense and consensus of logic, in order to contract certain right and just laws to protect the sovereignty of individual human beings and to preserve the sovereignty and dignity of individual human rights.

Tyranny has always wrongly demanded to assume a position of absolute authority and compelled and coerced others to be passive about their own existence—to live as if each does not rightly own one's own existence.

Tyranny only makes of other individuals mere subordinate objects in one's perceived ownership of a supreme and absolute version of reality—a version which only looks down upon other people as simple assets or as a mere resource to be exploited and devoured.

Tyranny strips others of their freedom, sovereignty, liberty, rights, dignity, and health, and it designates itself entitled to serve as owner and dictator over their bereft carcasses.

To the tyrant, other individuals are not sovereign beings at all; they are less than beings—they are pithy pieces of property, to be owned, controlled, and manipulated by the very wants, whims, wishes, and desires of the tyrant.

The tyrant wants all whom it encounters to conform and adhere to its prescribed and absolute uniform way of doing things—to all obey its impulsive and compulsive demands—to all abide by the same supreme way of living and perceiving things, which it has so conveniently commanded to dictate and lay down.

Tyranny is fueled by insecurity and driven by the physical want, emotional urge, and mythical desire to devour the will of any and all other individuals it here comes to encounter and to empower itself through the subjugation of others. It wants to impose a totalitarian will upon others. It means to wage war against the sovereignty of individuals and seek to dissolve the will of others into its perceived and supposed absolute and supreme wants, whims, wishes, and desires.

Tyranny seeks to subvert the meaning and value of sovereignty—to invade and overtake the will of other individuals.

In the case of physical or physically violent crimes—in cases such as murder, rape, assault, theft, arson, etc.—the tyrant overtakes the will and violates the rights of others in a more physical and physically violent way. Violations of sovereignty are there more explicit and obvious. One there overtakes the will of another individual in plain sight and assumes a position of ownership of some physical force of supremacy over others in a more tangible and explicit way.

One there violates sovereignty by *physically* overtaking ownership of another individual's life, body, property, etc.

But in forms such as bigotry, fascism, and despotism, tyranny instead violates sovereignty by assuming ownership of a more dubious "moral" supremacy over others, rather than a specifically physical one.

Tyranny here rather appoints itself to a position of absolute and supreme *moral* authority over others. It believes itself entitled to impose an absolute and supreme moral judgement against others—to grade or degrade the value of other individuals' interests, identity traits, or very *being* at all—those who might happen to be different than those of its own kind.

Tyranny in this way violates sovereignty and manifests itself in the role of the supremacist. It wants to impose supremacy over others—in contradiction to the interests of sovereignty.

In the interests of *supremacy*, an individual or group of individuals comes to assume or impose some form of ownership, dictatorship, or absolute authority over the sovereign identity, interests, and values of other individuals. One even often comes to assume to own a supreme set of moral rights over *all* others.

This then comes to shed light on the realization of why the notions of morals and morality have themselves always been so prone to corruption. Morals, in this sense, have too often been interpretted to mean to imply singular and supreme rights—where this particular identity trait or that particular interest or this particular custom comes to be graded as "*moral*", right, and superior, and subsequently, all other kinds are degraded as *immoral*, wrong, or inferior. It is the recognition here that morals have often proven to be little more than value judgements which have congealed together into the force and might of group supremacy upon a common trait, interest, custom, or belief. They have even been construed and imposed as demands to which all members of a particular society are often coerced, admonished, or even outright forced to adhere.

Where morals and morality could have and should have only ever been the simple respect and appreciation of the value of sovereignty between individuals, they instead became this sort of impetus of supremacy. Morals became applied as rigid, singular sets of prejudicial and domineering "rights" for all. Societies, cults, and factions then set about to wage war against one another to vye for moral supremacy and dominance of their particular kind.

These ways then are really just the lingering leftovers of the ancient world still festering in our modern appliances.

But this is not the ancient world anymore. Humanity should be way past the point of being stuck under those prejudices, presumptions, and presuppositions—oblivious to the fact that life is plenty more complex, diverse, and kinetic than that. We have all been introduced now. Humans have become acquainted with one another and all the various types and kinds of different identity traits, characteristics, interests, and values of many different and distinct individuals existing throughout the world. Unlike the ancient world, information now travels quickly. And we can travel quickly. We can now very easily move between different experiences and engage with all sorts of different ideas, interests, people, and places.

Unlike the ancient world, we are no longer compelled to spend our entire lives within the walls of the same sedentary settlement, stacking stones under the absolute authoritarian rule of the same sedentary and uniform set of tyrannical impulses and prejudices—isolated and removed from the rest of the world. Each is availed now to knowledge and awareness of many different interests, and each and every individual is rightly availed the sovereign freedom to navigate and find among so many different interests those in which one comes to relate and discover a true sense of self, a sense of agreement, and the gratifications of self-identity and self-awareness.

Each individual is then, to a certain extent, availed to become a sovereign collage of culture unto oneself.

About the identity traits, interests, and values of human beings, none has any such rightful claim to any such categorical and universal agreement as to which particular one kind of person should rightly own any such claim to be the supreme and absolute right kind over all others. From one individual to another, the identity traits, characteristics, interests, or values that will come to be known as rightly one's own will always and only inevitably vary.

In contrast then to the many tyrannies waged in the interests of supremacy, we evolve to realize and appreciate the real and true value of freedom—of the rightful sovereignty of individuals.

One sovereign individual does not here then rightly own any such absolute authority to grade or degrade the values of another individual's existence. Each is only rightly sovereign about the ownership of one's very own self, being, values, interests, responsibilities, and so forth. One individual's interests, values, or beliefs do not then rightly own any such jurisdiction over the being, values, beliefs, or interests of another sovereign individual.

Where *laws* are then to be rightly made—that is, with *logic*—they are to be made to respect the rightful sovereignty of individual human beings and the rightful sovereignty of individual identity, interests, and values—in contrast and opposition to the *supremacy* and tyrannies of believing one particular type or category supreme over another.

Where laws are to be made rightly, they are to be made with logic—to realize that each individual is a sovereign experience of being, and that what suits the tastes of some individuals may be thoroughly or completely foreign to others. And such laws would also be rightly made to realize that each individual should be availed the right to pursue such sovereign interests.

So then if any society, such as that of a nation, purports to be a *sovereign* nation, then it must only logically be a nation that promotes and encourages the value of sovereignty among its citizens. If a nation would otherwise claim to be a sovereign nation, while yet condoning or allowing acts of genocide, slavery, terrorism, or other types of human rights violations to occur within its borders, then such a nation would have no logical right to claim to be a nation of *sovereignty*.

Such a nation would be exhibiting no such interest in the value of sovereignty. Such a nation would rather be engaged in the interests of supremacy.

A nation cannot simply expect to count its mere "separateness" from other nations as validation to be called a sovereign nation. If it is truly a nation of sovereignty, then it must be a nation that values the sovereignty of its individual citizens as its paramount concern.

Otherwise, it is only concerned with supremacy and not sovereignty.

If a society of individuals, such as that of a nation, does come to convene and engage in the spirit of freedom, to uphold and appreciate the true sovereignty of all individual citizens, then such a society or nation would be right indeed to call itself a sovereign society or a sovereign nation—a society or a nation truly committed to the interests of freedom.

This is the crossroads where humanity is then, and this is where humanity has been for far too long—it is either sovereignty, freedom, and peace or it is supremacy, tyranny, and violence.

This is indicative of the fact that all absolute authoritarian and totalitarian societies, nations, regimes, cults, and other organizations are indeed made upon a very premise in contrast and contradiction to the value of freedom and the rightful sovereignty of individual human beings. They are predominantly only made in the interests of supremacy of one kind over another, and thus they only continue to facilitate the ways of tyranny.

But each individual human being is only rightly sovereign. Each is only right unto the sovereign ownership of one's own sovereign traits, values, and interests. No race, gender, creed, ethnicity, skin color, eye color, sexual orientation, heritage, interest, taste, tendency, preference, type of clothing, or culinary choices of Homo sapiens sapiens rightly reigns supreme over all others. None rightly represents what is right for all.

Each is here only rightly a distinct individual representative of human being, and all human beings ultimately stem from the same terrestrial origin. Whether from Ireland or Thailand, Norway or Zimbabwe, Costa Rica or Topeka, the South Pacific or the North Atlantic, West Virginia or East LA, the salt of the ground is earthly brown the world around. No one wins the battle for supremacy. No shade, tint, or hue of any land or any man, no trait, characteristic, or aspect of any individual's identity rightly ranks supreme to any other—and by the same respect, none is therefore inferior to any other.

We are only one species, and each is only one individual. There are currently over eight billion distinct representatives of Homo sapiens sapiens alive, and no individual is of any longer lineage or more special attachment to the evolution of the species or the planet than any other. We are all of the same earthly age of the same earthly species.

There are really only two logical distinctions that matter in a free society—the individual and the species. All distinctions in between are just facets of the tapestry of the individual. No attachment to any sense of group supremacy in between is of any sane or logical validation for violating the sovereignty of others. Each individual is only rightly sovereign about one's own self and one's own being.

Of sovereignty, individuals are free. Of supremacy, individuals are not free—they are rather only owned and controlled by some form of tyranny.

The Contract of Free Will

AND SO, BETWEEN ONE individual human being and another, there does indeed exist the necessity of a contract. And this contract is only rightly and logically to be made in the interests of freedom—in the interests of the sovereignty of the individual.

Freedom is a conceptual contract. It is a conscious agreement to attest to one's presence and attendance at the table of society as representative of a sole, sovereign, and independent individual human being.

One thus here neither rightly engages out of the impulses of truancy or tyranny—the very antitheses of freedom.

One only rightly sits at the table of society in a position of freedom—not in a position of captivity. One is neither rightly captor nor captured—as it is the *condition* of captivity that exists in opposition to freedom and not simply one particular vantage point or another.

Freedom is the value of paramount concern, in precedence to all other values. Even the value of equality loses its shine without the precedent and paramount value of freedom. By even introducing the value of equality at all, each is only there inherently attesting to the prior and precedent recognition of each's presence and existence as a rightly sovereign individual. If we are equal, then we are really only equal unto the value of individual sovereignty. We are equal insofar as each is rightly *one* sovereign individual.

One slave could easily be said "equal" to another, but what good would such equality serve them there? It is rather in fact towards the precedent and paramount value of freedom that individuals should rightly aspire.

Freedom is the value such that neither individual rightly imposes a position of supremacy over the other. And as such, neither party involved rightly falls to the position of slave or servant or master to another.

One individual does not rightly assume ownership over the life, body, mind, interests, values, identity traits, characteristics, etc. of any other individual. Each is only rightly representative of a sovereign and independent individual ownership of these rights. One individual owns no such right to force others to adopt his or her values and interests as their own, nor prevent others of different values and interests than one's own from the fundamental rights of life, liberty, and the pursuit of fulfillment.

No individual, nor any group of individuals rightly impedes any sovereign individual from pursuing their *own* sovereign rights and their *own* sovereign courses of interest. No person or organization rightly owns any such rightful jurisdiction to impose any such form of totalitarian rule over the rights of all other individuals.

Each individual is only logically and rightly sovereign unto one's own being, life, body, property, courses of interest, values, and responsibilities.

Against the many impulses of tyranny and truancy, the value of freedom is thus conceptualized to ripen and become fulfilled.

Human beings evolve to become sovereign individuals—to overcome the many phases of truancy—to overcome the refusal to grow up, to overcome the refusal to mature and evolve, to overcome the refusal to be responsible for oneself, to overcome the refusal to effort the means by which and through which one must rightly come to own and maintain the responsibilities conducive to being such a rightly sovereign and independent individual.

But all too often, individuals are led, and even encouraged to believe that the refusal to grow and mature and evolve *is* freedom. Individuals are told that when they reach the age of around eighteen years, they are adults and they are free. So many simply take this as validation to cease any further development, and the maturation process is thereby effectively put on pause—in many instances, for the duration of life.

But while this kind of consignment to being overruled by the commands and demands of impulses may serve another person in a position of power and supremacy looking for subordinates quite well, it serves the individual no such benefit.

The goal of individual freedom is essentially to reach a place in one's life where one breaks free from and surpasses the need to be dependent upon other authority figures in order to maintain the responsibilities of one's own being—where one becomes truly sovereign and independent and comes into one's own as one's own true authority figure—where one matures to know and govern oneself as a sovereign ownership of rights and a sovereign representative in society with other sovereign individuals.

Thus, no individual is rightly prevented, impeded, or held back from achieving such a course of growth, maturity, and sovereignty. No individual is rightly prevented, impeded, or denied opportunities and courses pursuant to life, liberty, and the pursuit of happiness on any grounds, let alone the grounds that some other individual or group of individuals has some sort of disagreement with some trait, characteristic, value, or interest of another individual.

So too then we evolve to overcome the many forces of tyranny which have long stood against the value and progress of freedom. Against the many archetypes of tyranny, the value of freedom has had to endure and must continue to strive to dispel.

Against all who wage war against the sovereignty of individuals, against all who stand opposed to freedom, the efforts towards the progress of freedom must continue to persevere and be dedicated to overcome.

A social contract then is not one rightly made in the interests of supremacy—as such only promotes a perpetual state of tyranny, conflict, and battles of will.

But to live and exist in day-to-day society should be no such constant battle. Contests and battles of will are rather designed to be made for a coliseum—where combatants consent to the sanctions of the sport to exercise and engage in a contest of will, where they compete for theatrical supremacy and dominance over their competitors.

A battle for supremacy and dominance might be natural for the ways of the wild—but for humans, it is only rightly made for theater and entertainment in an arena of consent, where competitors consent to the "battle" and spectators consent to watch and be entertained.

A free society and a right and just social contract are to be made of no such interest in violence and turmoil and bloodshed and battles for supremacy and dominance.

A free society is instead rightly made in the interests of sovereignty and independence—in the interests of freedom—where the sovereignty of each individual contributes to the sovereignty for all.

In a right and just society, in a right and just contract of society, the value of freedom is indeed paramount. In a right and just society, each individual stands as rightly representative of a sovereign will. Thus, none rightly holds supremacy and dominance over another.

In a free society, individuals are not rightly excluded from participation, deemed unfit, or denied civil liberties simply because other individuals decide to declare supremacy and dominance of some particular kind over others. No individual is rightly excluded from civil liberty or denied freedom on any such grounds.

It would seem absurd to want a society in which we would sit idle and think it normal and acceptable for a person to barge into a pizza parlor and demand that others be prevented from eating anchovies on their pizza because he finds anchovies to be yucky. A free society would not rightly want to allow a person to shut down the pizza parlor and throw everyone out because he believes anchovies are offensive to his taste. A free society would not rightly want to allow a person to prevent people who do eat anchovies on their pizza from enjoying civil and sovereign liberties because he finds anchovies not to his liking.

While this may sound like an absurd anecdote, consider that what happens in reality is actually much, much worse.

In reality, when certain individuals become obsessed with the physical want, emotional urge, and mythical desire to impose supremacy and dominance over other individuals, they barge into schools and businesses and public events and actually murder real human beings and destroy real human lives, in displays of the most vulgar and obscene violations of freedom.

And yet more and more individuals are becoming emboldened to engage in just such horrific acts. They have even become so audacious as to loudly and explicitly announce their plans to murder others because they are excited about the fact that many in society seem to want to look upon them and their loud and explicit intent as just another simple example of "freedom" at play.

It is these kinds of glaring misrepresentations and misconstructions of the concept of freedom that has brought us to this point. We are way too steeped in the habit of referring to acts of anti-freedom as acts of freedom. When an individual expresses a belief in supremacy and dominance over others and sets about to act upon this belief and impose such supremacy and dominance over others, far too many people have come to look upon *that* individual as being the one who is somehow exercising "freedom".

But where any belief or set of beliefs is designed to impose supremacy and dominance of a particular kind and condemn and desecrate the rights of other individuals, then it says something about the character of the individuals who authored those beliefs. It says nothing of any interest in freedom.

Actually, instead, it says very much to the contrary—it says very much in contempt of freedom.

And the perpetual cycle of supremacy, tyranny, and violence only then continues to plague the progress of humanity and human freedom.

All that sane, viable individual human beings have ever been striving for is the peace and prosperity of a life of sovereignty, freedom, and independence. The ills and horrors of individuals being made to feel like prisoners, slaves, and prey within this planet, within a country, within a town, within any society, within their own bodies, humans have only rightly sought to overcome.

And it has always been and continues to be the many forces of tyranny that have stood against the value of freedom and committed such atrocities against other human beings.

Relative to the evolution of the species, the evolution of the conscience, of consciousness, and of logic have only been relatively recent developments. And the recognition of the imperative and intrinsic value of freedom has only been an even more recent development. We have barely even begun to unlock and unleash the true potential of the species to evolve.

What is always lacking in society are opportunities and pathways to sovereignty. What is lacking is encouragement and education towards courses of sovereignty, independence, and maturity.

Individuals should only rightly be encouraged and educated towards a path of sovereignty, so that they may pursue courses consistent with their abilities and proclivities—so that each may indeed thereby come to fulfill one's own true sovereign potential and contribute one's best sovereign self and one's best sovereign efforts to one's society.

Instead, individuals are twisted and contorted into subordinate, subservient, and unfulfilling roles, drained of their willpower, and dragged through life in an expedited and repetitious cycle of stress, anxiety, angst, depression, and illness. For many, meaning and fulfillment in life is always kept two steps out of reach, much like a carrot at the end of a string. In this respect, the morning coffee is only placebo enough to make the hands on a clock turn just the slightest little bit faster.

Individuals are far too often hemmed in and steered down paths of abject servitude and left to fade away from their true selves and a real life of sovereignty. Supremacy and tyranny get in the way and drown out the availability of other opportunities which would otherwise be availed towards the sovereignty for all. The progress and improvements and opportunities for individuals to succeed are thus hindered, impeded, and diminished.

Here again, the voices of truancy will express frustration because what is really required towards any such improvement is effort. But humanity cannot rightly expect the progress of any individual or any society to improve if it continues to forego the steps necessary to encourage such progress simply because it sounds like too much effort. A society of individuals is indeed destined for failure if it believes it will benefit in any way in the long run by impeding the sovereignty, independence, and freedom of the individuals who constitute the society and by preventing such individuals from taking the steps necessary to engage the efforts to realize their fullest sovereign potential.

Freedom is a logical contract. It is the rightful logical contract of any right and just society. It is to live up to the true value of individual sovereignty, and thus in return, it inherently avails the value of freedom to others. And where others are more sovereign, more sovereignty is thus availed to you.

Each individual here then rightly comes to regard one another as sovereign and free, and the contract is thereby implied.

In the end, there is the will of the individual, and there is the value of freedom.

From the sovereignty of the individual to the sovereignty of a society, the true value of freedom is still waiting to be realized—